THEI

THERE ARE NO DEAD

A REFUTATION OF MORTALITY

First Edition 1912
Sophie Radford de Meissner

New Edition 2018
Edited by Tarl Warwick

COPYRIGHT AND DISCLAIMER

FOREWORD

For those interested in the topic of spiritualism the name Sophie de Meissner is hardly an unknown; this enigmatic socialite was born before the American Civil War and lived into the era of televisions and nuclear weapons having lived to 102 years of age. While she wrote a surprisingly large number of works, this is her one foray into the concept of the afterlife, and of mortality.

The title is fitting considering the conceptions spoken of here; literally, death being a sort of illusion, in which the continuation of consciousness and even pseudo-physicality is synchronized with death to such a degree that the dead individual has potential difficulty comprehending that they have died. The information here is in two parts; first, communication the author claims to have had with spirits, and secondly some various correspondence with other spiritualists and individuals at various times.

Altogether the work is quite good, although at times the spirits purportedly being contacted shift from one subject to another- there is even mention of politics and then-modern events, notably the sinking of the USS Titanic and war involving Russia.

This edition of "There Are No Dead" has been carefully edited and reformatted for modern standards. Care has been taken to retain all original intent and meaning.

THERE ARE NO DEAD

A PRAYER

Almighty God, the Father of our Lord Jesus Christ, who is the Resurrection and the Life, mercifully protect and guard the Souls of these Thy servants, whom Thou hast called to a grander and fuller Life with Thee.

Pardon and deliver them from all their sins, whether voluntary or involuntary; vouchsafe them all joy and happiness in the fulfillment of such righteous works as their freed spirits may be best fitted for, and grant them grace to perform Thy high and Holy missions with such fidelity that they may attain everlasting joy and bliss.

Unto us, O Lord, despite the glorious change that has come to them, accord a full and perfect trust in the nearness of their presence, and mercifully preserve us from every thought, word, or deed, which might cause them pain, or retard the moment of our once again beholding them when our own days here shall have been numbered. Bless and comfort, we beseech Thee, all who weep and suffer; and grant us grace so to order our lives here below, that when it shall please Thee to call us to Thy glorious Presence, we may be received into Thy Courts of Light, through the merits and mediation of Thy Most Blessed Son, Our Lord and Savior. Jesus Christ.

Amen.

FOREWORD TO THE 1912 EDITION

I have selected from among "Communications," that, coming to me, have extended over a period of well nigh fourteen years, such as would best illustrate the conditions governing the life upon the Higher Plane; but as no two lives in this world are identical, neither are any two upon the Plane Beyond, so, without further comment, I will simply show such things- or a very small part of such things- as have been told to me, trusting that they may bear a word of comfort to those who now sorrow as without hope for their own loved ones who have been called to the Grander Life Beyond.

In the following brief summary of the comfort and reassurance that has been vouchsafed me from the Beyond there is no attempt at anything in the way of "test" cases, despite the fact that many such have been shown me, though nether in reply to a demand for the same. Spontaneously things have been told me, either for my own guidance, or for that of friends in sorrow and despair; and spontaneously have I been informed of things that have afterward come to pass; but any attempt at forcing communications in regard to future happenings has invariably been met by a well deserved rebuke from those who are "given charge" over each and all of us.

This gift, of which St. Paul tells us in 1 Cor. xii, 10th verse, and which the Apostle to the Gentiles there denominates as "discerning of spirits," is one which was doubtless possessed in much greater degree in the early years of the Christian Era, when the followers of Jesus of Nazareth were taught to ascribe all that was helpful and uplifting to the working of the Divine Spirit, and were not afraid of boldly proclaiming that which had thus been shown them for their guidance. "Neglect not the gift that is in thee," writes St. Paul to Timothy, proving that Timothy, himself, was endued with a gift beyond that accorded to ordinary men for the service of the Lord. Such a gift should assuredly be cherished as a sacred trust, and never used in a spirit of mere idle curiosity. If properly made use of, it will prove helpful to many people.

It is strange that so many professing Christians exclaim against the possibility of Intercommunion between the seen and the Unseen, the temporal and the Eternal, since the Christian Church Itself is founded upon this very Inter-communion; and nowhere in the Scriptures are we told that this, or any other of the Gifts of the Spirit enumerated by St. Paul in I Cor. xii :10, were ever withdrawn from man. Can it be that we fear to know that our loved ones are happy in serving God, rather than spending eons of time in purposeless slumber? Which idea is in direct contradiction to Christ's own teaching. "We can know of such things only when we shall have passed through the Valley of the Shadow," assert many. Whence comes the authority for such an assertion?

Surely not from the words of our Lord, Who tells us: "God is not the God of the dead, but of the living." These words leave us, indeed, but one of two alternatives, namely; either God abandons those who have been taken from this world, or we have before us the glorious certitude that: THERE ARE NO DEAD.

THERE ARE NO DEAD

Peterhoff, near St. Petersburg, Russia, 4 A. M., August 29th, 1899. (Twelve hours after the dear Lord had called my blessed son from this world)

"Parly was with me at the end. He took me at once in his arms and told me not to be afraid, that all was well ; and so God helped me to pass into Life!"... "God helps us all at the end, they all say so here."

"Don't begrudge Parly his happiness."

(From my son.) Another voice: "He had never once left the right way. He had fulfilled his destiny faithfully, and that is the best thing of all. God needed him here. God has great work for him to do. Work for which there is no other one here so well fitted as is our darling boy."

"God has called me to a higher life. If you knew how happy we all are here you would not mind my having gone to comfort Parly, who was so very lonely 'till I came." (My son.)

(A friend) "God did not let him know he was so ill until he heard his own father calling him, then he was so delighted to see his father he forgot all else."

Q. "Was he frightened?"

A. "Not at all, at first, for we were all about him- those you love; then came a moment when he understood, and, at first, he was frightened," (later I was told that he was frightened at realizing that I was alone in the world) "but for a moment only, for God showed him happiness at once, and all was well with the

7

darling boy." (From my husband.)

"Yes, God showed me happiness at once, and so kept me from all fear."

Q. ("Was it on his father's account he was taken?")

A. "Yes, surely for that; but God has other and grander work for the boy to do, and you should be thankful that God called him for so high a purpose." (W.)

Tiflis, September 24, 1899. (His birthday) "God has blessed your boy above measure."

October 22nd, 1899. "There is no death, only a great and glorious change."

"You must go and tell people what God has shown you- God wishes you to do so."

Then there was some talk about praying for those who had been taken from this world, and I was told it helped them greatly.

Q. ("Is it harder for those for whom there are no prayers?")

A. "Yes, much harder for them to attain to happiness." (Thinking of the regiment, I am told:) "In danger oft he will be with them" and again: "God has saved your boy from terrible things."

Many of his comrades were killed in the Russo-Japanese war six years later, as, although this particular regiment, whose duty is the guarding of a part of Russia's southern frontier, did not go to the war, many of the officers were transferred to other regiments at their own request in order to take an active part in that great struggle.

After those first days I did not put down the things that were told me, although I was constantly guided in all I did by those in the Beyond, and it was not until June, 1901, that I find any certain record of the help that was and is always given me. But as this is not a relation of personal happenings but of communications telling of the Life Beyond, I will speak only of such things as could throw light upon the experiences of those who, having been called hence, have shown me what I was able to understand of their continued existence and surroundings. Any remarks I may wish to insert I will put in round brackets.

June 10th, 1901:

"Always use your own judgment about things, whatever may be told you."

"Ask whatever you will of heavenly things. Yes, our work is always to help one another- both those here, and those in the world. Many do not know they are no longer in the world for many days- even weeks."

("But they no longer see about them those whom they knew in this life.")

"Yes, they do, for their Spirits are often here."

("When they sleep?")

"Yes, and also when they are awake. Your Spirit is here so often with us when you are wide awake. Yes- your Spirit is also absent (from your body) in the world- it is more often in

9

Russia than where you are- that is because it knows your work is there- so very soon now- and it seeks to prepare the way for you."

August 3rd:

"Our occupations? Yes; we have music so beautiful you cannot even imagine what it is like- but we have every other occupation, too, just as on the earth. Yes, even horses to ride." (II Kings vi, 17). "Dandy is such a good little dog, and he is always with Parly, or with me. Yes- a most beautiful river with boats or swimming, as one likes. Yes- I have plenty of young comrades here whom I have known before, though not all in my last existence in the world."

("Then we do return here several times?")

"Most of us, yes- but I thank God we shall not have to go back there again."

("Then one is working out their redemption there also?")

"Most surely that is always going on!"

August, 1901:

In reading of the Boers, I am told- "Of the remaining few a great nation will be formed." (K. F.)

"We all have our houses here, of course. Parly and I and... All is so congenial- the others are near by- Grandpa and my uncles and aunts. Yes- there are artisans and decorators here for the houses just as in the world. You know how Parly and I always loved Dickens' Pickwick- well- Dickens is here, and we hear him lecture often- so very well..."

THERE ARE NO DEAD

"There is very much to tell- You all think so wrongly of the life here- it differs so little from that in the world, except in that it is so much more grand and full."

August 10th

Today we may not tell you of earthly things; only of our life here. Yes- I go rowing and swimming both in the beautiful river- and I ride on horseback also- Yes, Parly rode so well always, and we ride so much together."

("But that is not at all according to the ideas they have here of heaven.")

"No- in the world they have no idea at all of what it is like in the World Beyond. Yes- when you are with us we walk together, and sit and talk on a lovely bank with such beautiful flowers all about."

August 14th

(We spend the day at Lake St. Catherine, North Granville, and there I am told:) "Yes, it is a lovely tranquil day- the last tranquil day for some time." (That evening I received a letter from my brother in Washington, saying thieves had broken into my Mother's house, and another from a niece saying she was going out to Manila to teach- a project she fortunately abandoned.)

August 15th:

"E- will not go to Manila. Tell her she cannot go- her father says so." (Her father had passed to the Life Beyond, and shortly after this the project was abandoned.) It was about this time when a sister of this same niece, one who had been taken

11

from this world when but a child of three years, gave me a beautiful picture of child life in the World Beyond. Thinking that at the time of her taking hence no member of her own family had as yet crossed the Borderline, I asked whether she had not been lonely just at first.

"Oh, not at all," she answered, "for our Savior took me at once with him. He takes all the little ones and keeps them with Him until they are strong enough to have work given them. Then they are always shown where He is to pass on His wonderful rounds of mercy and we all run and wait for Him and He speaks to us always as He passes by and we are all as glad and happy as we can be and we thank and bless our Heavenly Father for having called us here so young as the Savior Himself takes care of us and that is the very best thing of all," Then she added: "Never think of me as a little girl now for I am very tall- taller even than Edith (her younger sister who was then about eighteen years old, while Eleanor herself who was speaking would have been about twenty) and she is a pretty tall woman. This is from Eleanor, your niece who prays for you."

August 16th:

We are extremely busy- yes- helping others, and beside that seeing such beautiful things ourselves. Yes, our house is most lovely. Surely, you will be with us always. We would like so much to show it to you- perhaps in a dream. You remember seeing Parly the other night in that- car- yes- traveling through space"; (this was in relation to a most impressive dream, or vision, I had had, in which I had conversed of many things of deepest interest with my husband). "K. F. was there, too, and others."

(One of my brothers- speaking from the Beyond) "I see Papa- he is sad just now because he knows you must soon leave

THERE ARE NO DEAD

Mamma, and she will be unhappy all the time again. No, you cannot do otherwise; but pray it may not be too long before you come to see her- hardly as soon as next spring."

(I sailed for Russia the first of the following February, but had not known the previous Summer that I should be able to go.)

August 17th:

"There will be a great change soon in your life."

August 18th:

"Ask us of our life here today. We went to a most beautiful service in the open air where a man preached of Our Lord's love and pity for all creation. All days are one to us here, for all are dedicated to the Lord- and so it should be on the earth. Yes, everything you do should be undertaken in the Name of Our Lord and Savior- nothing is trivial."

(Just here I would insert a quotation from a letter of Doctor Richard Hodgson's, dated March 18th, 1901, to whom I had written of some communication as being trivial. "You need not be apprehensive that anything should appear 'trivial.' Even the falling leaf may be a clue to gravitation.")

"Yes- the service was held under the trees, there was music such as you cannot imagine. Yes- all sang; but there was also a choir of angels. After the service we walked by the beautiful river and saw all our friends and acquaintances- all those whom you know, and Parly's family whom you never knew. Yes, God let them all come together to meet me at my coming- it was so beautiful, only we were sad because you cried so then. No, you could not help it; that was why God let us go to

13

you at once. Yes, we think of you always, and wish you were with us; but God will not let you come 'till you have finished your work. God will let you help many, many people, and we will always be near you."

August 22nd:

"Be very careful and tender with your dear Mother, for you will have to leave her soon now." (From my Father)

(At that time I saw no special reason for my going to Russia- nor did I see how I could afford it.)

"Pray for perfect Faith and Love that casteth out all fear- it is difficult, but not unattainable."

"We are all so happy together- you would hardly understand some things; but we are all so busy, principally at first receiving the newcomers- after that we pass on..." (from a friend).

August 25th:

Here we have two languages- the spoken and 'thought' language which is beautiful beyond anything you can imagine- the first is used by the newcomers, the other later."

August 27th:

"We may not tell you of earthly things today. Yes, we feel always so strongly the Presence of Our Lord and Savior, Jesus Christ- and many see Him. I hope now to see Our Blessed Lord soon. Yes, we are always most deeply conscious of His Presence. Of course- ask that- Our Lord and Savior is a Most Personal God, and our only hope of Salvation. Yes, all must

14

return to the earth until they learn to know and reverence His Name."

August 28th:

Every day we have the same beautiful service in the beautiful gardens- then always walk by the river- and then have so much to do both here and in the world- then Parly and I row often on the river. I row and he steers, just as in the world. Yes- very easy- the boat glides almost of itself; then we swim also. Yes, the water is clear as glass, or crystal, or sunlight itself. Yes, we are often in the house, and sit there talking over all these beautiful things. Ask about the afternoons- we meet in the beautiful gardens and pick such exquisite flowers. No- they never fade. We put them in vases. Yes, most beautiful flowers are about the houses, and even inside" (the houses) "too. We are most happy; but there are always greater heights to attain- so pray- yes, yes, pray that we may see Our Lord and Savior, that is the best thing of all- pray for that."

"The children dance here, and are so gay and happy; even those who have none of their family- for then Our Savior, Himself, takes them."

"There is no night here- what you call the night is the best time of all, for then you are with us. As soon as you are asleep your Spirit is here, and we sit and talk either in the house or in beautiful gardens, or on the river's brink."

August 30th:

"We were both so happy yesterday- Our Lord and Savior was with us all the day..." (here was given a description of Christ's first appearance to them which I could not attempt to put into words, but which closed in the following manner:)

THERE ARE NO DEAD

"After that we knew that nothing could ever be wrong again! Ask of today. This morning we have been to a most beautiful service where a sermon was delivered on Our Lord's Life and work while in the world by one of those who was in the world at that time- he told of all the anguish and pain He endured for the human race- it was so touching we could not but weep, and yet so lovely we could not be sad- after that Our Savior Himself spoke to us in His Grand and loving way. He was with us all the day yesterday, and this morning, too. No, there is no day and night here- it is all one."

September 1st:

The language here is what you would call telepathy- but there is still another language infinitely more beautiful- yes, a thought language, of course."

September 7th:

"Our work has greatly enlarged since the day you prayed for us to see Our Savior. You helped us to attain another step- God would never let us forget to pray for you even if we could do so, which we could not."

(In reading of unceasing prayer, I think: "Yet one must turn the mind sometimes to earthly matters?")

"Yes; but immediately afterwards think again of Our Heavenly Father's unceasing care for you, and then God will be able to help you so very much."

September 10th:

"Yes, we are now at the beautiful service which is held every day- according to your count- between twelve and one o'clock. Yes, we can speak as well, even better then than at other times. Yes, they must stay" (in the world) "until they believe in the Divinity of Our Lord and Savior- pray for them, there are some who have crossed the Borderland who cannot yet understand. We wanted you to read that book- the lesson it taught you was proved by what you prayed for today." (strengthening of will power).

September 12th:

Yes- God has taken, and takes, such good care of me now, and did also in the earth life, though I never understood that 'til I came here- even in the manner of my coming for I knew nothing until happiness was shown me, and so was never frightened. Yes, many are frightened; those who do not believe in the Name of Our Lord and Savior Jesus Christ but so many do believe- and they are so happy."

("How about those who have wanted to believe but thought they could not do so?")

"Those will be so unhappy at first, because they have so misunderstood; but they will soon learn, as they are so in earnest."

September 15th:

"We are at the beautiful service now; it is more beautiful than ever, for now Our Lord and Savior is always with us- we have passed... attained a higher plane."

September 16th:

"There is a great crisis approaching soon in Russia." (this was three years before the outbreak of the Russo-Japanese war).

September 26th:

"We have always the beautiful services which are so peaceful and comforting."

September 29th:

"We have seen Grandpa R- a great deal these past days, he is always happy, though sad just now to think you must so soon leave dear Grandma."

October 1st:

We may tell you only of earthly things today, because your thoughts are fixed on those. No, you cannot help it, for there are such important things now"- (I was waiting to hear from Miss Elizabeth Marbury in regard to Count Tolstoy's play "Ivan the Terrible," which I had translated and sent to her to be placed)- "write at once to Miss Marbury" (asking her) "to return you a copy- ask Mrs. L- about Mansfield, no, you cannot write to him yourself, but Mrs. L- might speak to him about it for you." (all of this came to pass within a month after this advice was given me, with the result that it was Mr. Mansfield who produced the play in question).

(On awaking at six a. m., October 1st, I wondered why I could not fix in my mind an image of Our Savior, and thought, "I must find an engraving that I like, and buy it for my room.")

Am told: "No, that is not the correct way."

(Q. "Why can I not form the picture in my mind?")

THERE ARE NO DEAD

A. "Because you cannot yet attain to that."

(Q. "How does one hold a Holy thought in mind?")

A. "Fix your thoughts first on some good man who is in the world."

(Q. "Will H. D. do?")

A. "For the moment."

(Q. "But I do not know what he looks like.")

A. "You do not need to know that; think of his writings."

(Q. "That is too general- I cannot recall them sufficiently distinctly.")

A. "Because you do not read in the right way. Read the article over carefully and attentively; then put down the book and go over the entire article mentally- recalling each point- and should you forget any one take up the book again and re-read that part, and you will soon find what a very different memory you will have. Do this each day for a short while, and you will soon perceive the benefit."

(To my great regret I must say that I was unable to follow this advice at that time.)

October 2nd:

(From my Mother's father, who had passed to the Beyond.) "It is astonishing how much your dear Grandmother resembles you- your Spiritual body of course, we only see that. Yes, this great movement is now preparing, and we will help you to be of service in it. Yes, we were always there when (your son) told you of the wonderful life here."

October 5th:

(From my son.) "We are to have such a beautiful service at noon; think of us then- Parly and I are always together, even though we have such different work to do. He goes to the earth much more than I. Yes, the work here is infinitely more beautiful. Yes, there are companies to be organized, soldiers of Christ, then we talk with higher Spirits who have attained to more glorious spheres- that is beautiful- and we sing in chorus, for God has taught me to sing as you can't imagine." (Russian men are, as a rule, musical, and when in the Cavalry School my son played often on the mandolin and balalaika together with his comrades.) "I always liked that too- No, we can't tell you of the other stars as yet, for all has not been shown us. There is so much to learn, and it is all so interesting. We can't tell you of Tiflis" (where his regiment is stationed) "but you will soon arrange about the tombstone- it must all be put in order because of the regiment." (That I was able to carry out the following Spring.)

October 6th:

(After coming from open air service at St. Alban's, Washington.) "We were all with you at the beautiful service this afternoon- it was something like our services here."

October 7th:

"There is so much to tell you of the life here- (it is) beyond anything you can imagine Yes, we go about and see such wonderful things; we ride and drive in beautiful cars- No, we do not always wish to be immediately at our destination, for there is so much to be seen in traveling through space. Yes, you were with us one night in one of these cars" (the vision of which I spoke) "we were all there, but you only saw Parly- you were so happy Edmund" (one of my brothers) "is here and wants to speak to you- There is so much to tell you- of previous existence. The Spirit existed long ages before the earthly body" (Sin.)- Yes, it is by the earthly existence we expiate that, it will all be overcome by prayer, by faith, and by Spiritual striving.

We all know why we return to the earth. I asked to go the last time- I chose that manner of expiation." (he was a cripple, and was taken from this world on his 16th birthday after years of terrible suffering.) "Pray for C-" (another brother) "and for me, that we may not have to return there again. No, no one wishes to go there except in expiation. You will be able to help so many to understand- it is so strange to us people do not understand, but many will."

October 10th:

(From Mrs. W-, a friend in the Spiritual world.) "I see S-" (my son) "and your husband a great deal. S- tells me of what you do and say in the world, and it interests me so. Yes, I am immensely interested in this Spiritual movement; it is so beautiful to know there will be more faith and more knowledge of the truth. Write to me often; S- will let me know when you want to do so."

October 11th:

"We may tell you only of our life here today. Yes, we are now at the beautiful service under the splendid trees, and Our Lord Himself is teaching us of how to help those in the world and those here, too. Yes, there are all degrees of happiness. Some do not understand- they are not developed; but soon they will do so, for the movement of which we told you will be here as well as on the earth- all originates here."

October 12th:

(From K. F.) "My good friend- something very important in your life will be decided tomorrow"- (within a few weeks after this Mr. Mansfield accepted my translation of "Ivan the Terrible," but I do not recall anything taking place on the day indicated.)

October 13th:

"We were with you at the service today- here we had the most beautiful service that has yet been, for Our Lord Himself spoke to us of His Life upon earth, and of all the grief and anguish He endured for humanity. It was most sad, but beautiful beyond words to describe. Then we sang as we have never sung before, for now the Angels themselves have taught us- and they sing with us, too, now."

October 17th:

We can tell you only of our life here today. The service was the most beautiful we have had yet, for Our Lord and Savior told us of His sufferings in the world for all mankind- it was so beautiful we all wept with joy and happiness. Then we sang such hymns of praise as you cannot even imagine in the world- hymns the Archangels have taught us. Yes, all were there whom you knew and loved in the world, and whom you know still better now they are in the World Beyond. Yes, Conrad" (the son of a dear friend of mine who was taken from this world six months after my son was called hence) "and I are a great deal together- we have many tastes in common, though he led a less active life than I, but he was more studious, much more. Yes, Parly and I have many tastes in common- we ride, and row, and swim so much together- each one does according to his taste, for we have many amusements here. Yesterday afternoon we were in the world for some time- then helping others here- and studying with the Archangels, they teach us such beautiful things. No, I did not care much for study there, but here it is so much more beautiful."

October 21st:

We cannot say any more about earthly things until you shall have heard of what is to be- don't go to that Court again"- (the Admiral Schley investigation)- "it is a great to do for nothing; they are both brave men, but it will end by people thinking Sampson is not a brave man, and that will not be right either."

October 22nd:

(From Captain E-, a Russian Naval officer who had left this world)- "I am so happy, but everything is so very different from what I had expected- all is so much more as it is in the world, so much more congenial, so infinitely more beautiful- if you could but tell my wife. I see your dear son, and my friend, they were the first ones I saw upon coming here. It was good to see old friends. Your Spirit had warned them of my coming, and so they came to meet me."

October 23rd:

(I am told that cremation causes often "awful suffering" in the Beyond.)

"The reason it causes such awful suffering in undeveloped natures is that it comes so shortly after the change called death- when the Spirit has not realized its separation from the body- as for the natural decomposition of the body- as that comes later and more gradually, the Spirit has had time to accustom itself to its new environment and to have lost all connection with the body, so that the natural manner of dissolution may affect it in no wise at all. Of course all highly developed Spirits lose this connection immediately, but there are so few, in comparison, of those now."

November 1st:

(From my son) "There is not much to say today. Yes, we have always the same beautiful services which grow more and more beautiful."

November 2nd:

"Get ready to return to Russia. You must go, even if things appear difficult."

(In reading a book of Professor Hyslop's, I mentioned 'Rector's' name aloud, and he at once responds :)

"Yes; I am here- do you want anything?"

(I tell him of how K. F. had told me I would be able to help others, and add that I cannot see just how that may be.)

A. "You will know in a few weeks. You will be much stronger, and will see them soon. It will come by prayer and fasting- to prepare your Spirit for this blessing- the time will be shown you. You will not be nervous, ever after that."

November 3rd:

"Mamma, ask us of the beautiful service here. It was the

most beautiful yet today, as Our Lord and Savior told us once more of His pain and sufferings in the world. We were so sad and yet so happy. All you love were there under the great, beautiful trees. You will soon be going to Russia; get all your things ready, don't worry about money- all is well now."

November 5th:

"Ask us only of our life here today. There is so much beside the beautiful service. We have been in the world this morning, especially in Tiflis- where you must go so soon now." (I did not go to Tiflis until June, 1905)- "tell them all" (the comrades) "about me, even of the riding, so it will not seem so strange to them- for it is not strange at all the life, just as the life upon the earth only so infinitely more beautiful. No, there is no such thing as jealousy, but all strive together for the general good."

November 7th:

Your Father is here"- (from my father)- God will show you what is His Blessed Will. Your mother will be unhappy for some months, but you will return within a year from the time you go." (I sailed February 1st, and returned the following November.)

("Shall I return to stay?")

A. "No."

November 14th:

(From K. F.) "It is all right about the lecture. We will all help you to help the dear little Church." (a lecture I was giving in aid of St. Alban's Chancel fund). "My good and true friend, you will help me very much in making known so many things to others, and to my dear friend, L. W."

November 18th:

(From a Spirit unknown to me) "Go today to Mrs. L-'s, and ask how you could see Mansfield, the rest will be shown you. No, you cannot understand work here which you will not be able to fulfill"- (meaning I must not turn my mind to things other than those intended for me to do)

November 19th:

(From my son) "Do not be discouraged if you do not hear from Mansfield for another day or two, as all will be arranged before he leaves Washington." (Mr. Mansfield took the manuscript of "Ivan the Terrible" before leaving Washington that week; and, according to the statement of his manager, Mr. Palmer, was studying the role of "Ivan" before he had had the play twenty-four hours in his possession.)

November 28th:

"Christmas will not be entirely happy as your dear Mother will be sad about your going- not till after January 1st."

December 10th:

"Your mind must not be so preoccupied else we cannot write."

December 15th:

(After listening to a sermon on the Second Coming of Our Lord.) "As each heart awakens to the Indwelling Spirit of

THERE ARE NO DEAD

Christ- that is the Second Coming of Our Lord." (Prepare ye the way of the Lord.)

"Yes; for each heart must be taught until the awakening comes."

("There is no Second bodily coming to the earth?")

"No- that is not the meaning of the text at all."

"Yes- there will be the preaching to all in the Beyond- but many will not be able to receive" (understand) "that teaching, and so will have to return to earth to learn of Our Lord and Savior Jesus Christ."

(In answer to the words; "It would be better for all the sick babies in the hospital to be taken from the world")

"No, surely not; for it is in this world alone that advancement can be accomplished, and so- were they taken away so soon- they would all have to return." (Yet in Heaven their Angels do always behold the Face of the Father?) "That is so- yet still they would have to return to fulfill their destiny, and to perfect themselves for higher Spheres"- (made perfect through suffering.)

December 27th:

"Be brave and strong."

December 31st:

"God will show you tomorrow what is His Blessed Will."

THERE ARE NO DEAD

January 2nd-3rd, 1902:

(Was in New York to talk over business matters with Mr. Mansfield.)

January 22nd:

Be brave and strong, and remember it is God's Will that you should go. He will protect you, and guard you from all harm and evil." (Sailed from New York February 1st, 1902, for Hamburg, after having signed contract with Mr. Mansfield for the production of the play "Ivan the Terrible," and received from him an advance sum on the representations- hence "their" telling me "not to worry about money matters" was fulfilled.) Just here I will tell of an incident concerning my sailing at that date which will serve to illustrate the guidance given me. About ten days before that time I had been told to engage my stateroom by the Hamburg line for the first of February, and I had made all my plans in accordance with this counsel. As certain money I receive from Russia was due January 28th, or 29th, I put all the rest I wished to take with me in a draft on St. Petersburg, counting upon the receipt of that from Russia for my journey. The 28th of January came and the money did not arrive, nor did it come upon the 29th or 30th. On Friday, January, 31st, the family advised me to telegraph to the ship and give up the stateroom, but I was told that I would sail the following day; and to the maid who inquired whether she must continue my packing or no, I said: "Go on with the packing. Get all my things ready."

After lunch I went to my room to take a rest, and had hardly dropped into a sound sleep before I was awakened with quite a start, and as I sat up, rather bewildered, I was told : "Dress yourself quickly and go to the bank." Looking at my watch I saw that it was five minutes after two o'clock, and as the bank closes at three I made a hurried toilet and reached 'Riggs

THERE ARE NO DEAD

Bank' just two minutes before closing time. I had no idea what I had gone there for, but as my draft on Russia was still there I went in and asked whether they could not exchange it and return me the money. "Certainly," replied Mr, B- "I can give it to you on Monday." At that time they had to send to New York for foreign drafts. "That will never do," I replied. "Give it to me as it is- I want to sail tomorrow morning."

"Of course you cannot do that!" remarked Mr. B-, impressively, as he handed me the draft. As I left the Bank the doors were closed behind me, and I stood there wondering what I should do next. "Go at once to the Russian Embassy," I was told. But at this I protested; if I had placed myself in a difficult position I was not going to the Embassy to ask for their assistance, therefore, instead of following this advice, which would have saved me endless trouble, I returned to my Mother's home on 30th and "P" Streets. Nothing had come, and so things went on until, just as the clock struck six, the door bell rang, and I heard one of the Embassy servants inquire for me. When I went down stairs he handed me a letter from Count Cassini askingn me to take a certain little package to his sister in law in Russia, and enclosing a draft for the looked-for money. Sending word that I should be at the Embassy immediately, I put on my hat and started out in the beginning of a snowstorm.

Fortunately I found a herdic, 'and when I reached the Embassy I was met by Count Cassini with the words: "Oh, Madame, if you had only come in two hours earlier! The secretaries have all left, and taken their keys with them, otherwise it would have given me great pleasure to cash that draft for you."

The upshot of the matter was that the Russian Ambassador finally handed me the sum in question, taking it in part from his own pocket and in part from the pockets of the members of his family and household- and here I was giving all this trouble, simply because I had not wished to follow the advice of those appointed to aid me. I left at midnight for New York, and sailed the following morning at ten o'clock. Wishing to show all sides of this momentous question, meaning of course in so far as they have been shown to me, I will tell of still one other occasion among the many when I have been aided by "their" counsel to arrange and decide my plans.

It was nearing the end of the month of August, 1906, immediately after the close of the Russo-Japanese war, and my niece Miss Edith Coyle (now Mrs. Francois Matthes) and I were preparing to leave St. Petersburg for a two months' stay in Germany before sailing for the United States. Having passed a strenuous period of a year and eight months in Russia we wished to find some quiet spot where undisturbed by social duties, we might spend our days in a dolce for niente under the shade of forest trees.

With this end in view I had written to many different resorts in Northern Germany only to receive in reply glowing descriptions of the many social attractions each place afforded. We had come to within a week of the first of September, the date fixed for our departure, and still were without any settled plans as to our destination, so that we could not even write to our friends and family in the United States as to where to address our letters. Upon awaking one morning at this time and realizing that we had but one short week before us in which to determine on our plans, I, in desperation, said to myself: "Something must be decided upon today."

"You must go to Munich," said my invisible guides in reply. To say that I was startled at this would but faintly express my feelings. Munich! "They" wished us to go to the Southernmost part of Germany when I was looking for something in the vicinity of Hamburg, from which port we were to sail. Furthermore I objected: "But I do not wish to go to a city. I am looking for some place in the country where we shall have pine forests in which to stroll."

"You will not be in Munich itself, but in the environs of the cit." I was told.

"How shall I know about this?" I inquired.

"Go today at four o'clock and call on Mrs. M-" came the answer.

Mrs. M- was the wife of an American engineer, who had recently come to St. Petersburg to take charge of an electric street car line which was in process of construction, and I had met her but some two or three times. She had called upon me and had then distinctly stated that she took her daily walk in the early afternoon and was never at home before five o'clock. In what manner she could have to do with my journey to Munich I could in no wise see, but, in accordance with the counsel given me, I called at the appointed hour and was immediately ushered into the drawing room where sat the lady in question. Having settled it in my own mind that I had been sent there in order to borrow a Baedecker- one of which I did not possess- I inquired, after exchanging a few remarks, whether she had one she could lend me, adding that I was thinking of going to Munich and wanted to look up our route. "Munich!" she exclaimed, rising suddenly, "Why, I have something much better than a Baedecker," and going to a door she opened it and called "Charles, come in here."

A moment later there appeared in the doorway a scholarly looking man whom the hostess introduced as "Professor X of Cornell"- the University of which both Mr. and Mrs. M- were graduates, and my fair young friend continued gaily: "Professor X has just this moment arrived direct from Munich and he can tell you all about it." This proved to be literally the case, and it was on the strength of the information then and there received that my niece and I found our way to an enchanting spot called "Grunwald," twenty minutes distant from Munich where, in the heart of a wonderful forest, we spent two perfect, never to be forgotten, months.

St. Petersburg, April 19th, 1902:

(In watching soldiers pass on their way to a parade, am told :)

"They will have other work before them before the summer is over- oh, most serious,- most serious for all the whole country. No, you cannot stay." (The question of time is, I am always told, the most difficult of all for them to explain. They see pictured before them events fulfilled, but the road that leads to the fulfillment is not shown them. Hence "before the summer is over" became a period of three years.)

St. Petersburg, May 8th, 1902:

(A very wonderful thing came to me this morning. In thinking that Pilate must have seen some glimpses of the Divine Glory, I am told:) "Before God I never saw that;"- (and in pondering on the words; 'Have thou nothing to do with that Just Man,' I hear, from Pilate's wife)- "That was the message I sent."

(From Simon the Cyrenian, who bore the cross)- "Oh, had I but known then of the wondrous blessing that was accorded me." (From the penitent thief)- "Yes, God has allowed of my becoming a helper in the Great Work of the Redemption." (From Mary Magdalene.)

THERE ARE NO DEAD

"God will help you- even as Our Lord and Saviour Jesus Christ helped me."

(Thinking on the words: "If I will that he tarry till I come, what is that to thee.?" I am told :) "God will help you to understand those words even as He helped me to understand them long afterwards, and when I was no longer of the world."

(Q. "Is it possible that St. John himself speaks to me?")

A. "Why not, since Our Lord and Savior Himself speaks to thee.?"

Friday, May 26th:

(I am told by One whose Name is above every name:)-

"I will help thee, my child."

Tuesday:

(From Pilate's wife)- "You must know that I am beside you each time you pray for me. Yes, it is praying for me when you think of me in connection with Our Divine Lord and Savior."

(From Barabbas)- "Oh, how terrible was that moment when they chose me in preference to that Divine One, Whose Glory was revealed to me so soon after that, and I was called to be a helper in the great work of the Redemption also."

(From the other thief upon the Cross:) "Oh, had I, too, but known Who it was suffering such agony in our company! My lot was the hardest of all who reviled Our Savior in that terrible time, because it was when he was passing from this world of sin that I chose to do so; for me there seems to be no hope."

Q. "You did not hear then Our Savior's words; 'Father, forgive them, for they know not what they do?"

"Oh, yes! Those words alone will lead us to the Light, but at the time I paid no heed to them."

(From the Blessed Virgin Mother:) "God will not allow me to be always beside thee, my child; but when there is necessity, know that I am near thee."

Wednesday morning:

(Thinking upon the words: "Barabbas was a robber," I am told:)

"Yes, once! but now a worker in the great army of the Redemption."

"Nothing more may be told you until you shall have written what was told you yesterday- henceforth note everything important that is said to you- else how can you show it unto others?"

May 20th, 1902:

(On looking from the window upon the decorations put up in honor of the visit of the president of the French Republic, M. Loubet, and noting the rain falling, I am told:)—- "This great friendship with France will not last more than one month longer."

(Q. "But France is Russia's only friend.")

THERE ARE NO DEAD

A. "Russia will not need any friend outside her own boundaries, for God will greatly increase her greatness- for the good of the whole world."

May 22nd:

(Watching the passing of President Loubet, am told once again:)

"Before one month all this will be at an end, and Russia will stand alone, but God will greatly increase her strength and greatness."

(History shows in how short a time the first part of this prediction was fulfilled.)

June 7th:

"S- must live with you entirely one day" (this alludes to a niece of mine who was at that date seven years of age.)

Peterhoff, July 6th:

(In Church) "Be brave, my child, for God will faithfully fulfill all the promises that have been made to you."

July 20th:

(From the Roman soldier who gave the sponge dipped in vinegar to Our Lord) "Oh, how I pitied those three poor men hanging upon the Cross, though I could not know that One was the Savior of the World- God has rewarded me most wondrously for that most simple act."

(In thinking of a very vivid dream that had come to me

shortly before my son was taken from the world, the significance
of which had always puzzled me, I am told: "The child who went
on in the boat was his earthly self, and the young man who stood
beside you was the Spirit of the Guardian Angel, who is now
about you ever."

(In the dream my son and I were, with many others, in a
boat on the River Aare in Switzerland, and stopping at one bank,
we stepped ashore, and he took my hand in his and we almost
ran up a narrow path leading to a peak high above the river.
Turning then and looking down, we saw the boat dashing along
the foaming torrent toward some seething rapids below, and in it
an old man at the helm and standing alone in the middle of the
boat my son, as at the age of three years, with his golden curls
and little white dress such as he had then worn. I awakened in an
agony of fear at knowing he must be dashed to pieces in the
seething whirlpool beyond, notwithstanding the fact that in this
vision my son, himself, in his Cavalry uniform, stood beside me
holding my hand in his.)

(Having secured the designs for the costumes for the
play of "Ivan," as well as a beautiful set of hand-colored
photographs from which the scenery was afterward copied, and
having furthermore translated from the Russian, during my stay
in St. Petersburg, the second play of Count Tolstoy's famous
Trilogy, "The Tzar Feodor," I took a steamer for New York,
leaving Hamburg, in the early part of November, 1902.)

Washington, December 2nd:

On hearing of a certain woman physician, who said she
was frequently asked by those in the Unseen to prescribe for
them, I was told: "It is not that they are really ill, but that
they do not realize that they have left their earthly" bodies. It is
for the same reason that we told you cremation caused such

suffering."

(Touching the subject of cremation:) "There are many who would not be affected by it, but there are also many who would, and as you cannot know which are the ones who would suffer, it is best to avoid it altogether."

December 13th:

"Our Savior's natural body was raised because it had Itself become wholly Spiritualized in serving as the Temple of the Incarnate God." and "The Holy Scriptures are inspired by the Divine Spirit."

(In speaking of the Life of the World to come, I am told:) "It is all one Life. Hell is a condition of the Spirit, which, seeing no way by which it can be saved from its sins, is plunged in the darkest despair- unrepentant of course- as, once repentance has begun, the darkness vanishes, and hell is passed away. The hardest work of all, and the most strenuous was (that done) during those three days when His earthly body lay in the tomb, for Our Lord was working then to save all those who had preceded Him upon the earth. His coming in human form, of course."

(Q. "Did Gamaliel live to see St. Paul become the great teacher he was.?")

A. "No." (I have since read that Gamaliel passed from this world in the year 44 or 45, which would be about the time St. Paul began his ministry.)

Q. "Could he follow him in his teachings from the Beyond?")

THERE ARE NO DEAD

A. "He had a greater teacher there- he had advocated justice in regard to Our Lord and Savior's followers (Acts V, 34-39). And so Our Lord has taught him Himself- that is of all things the most beautiful!" Matt. XX, 14- "I will give unto this last even as unto thee?"

"It is a question of greater or less fidelity in their work- not a question of time."

March 29th, 1903:

"This brief stay upon the earth is but an episode in Life's grand progressive whole."

(Q. "What is the meaning of the words; 'For in death there is no remembrance of Thee'?") (Ps. VI, 5.)

A. "Death is here used as a synonym for 'sin'- and in 'sin' no man remembereth the Lord. Time here is reckoned by achievement."

April 18th, 1903:

(On reading an article about Mormonism, I am told ;)

"That is the crevice which will become a yawning chasm, and overturn the government of this country. "Raise the dead'- Recall sinners to the way of Life."

April, 1903:

"There will be great, changes in Russia soon- great disorders, but those days will be shortened. And then will come a period of great prosperity." (This was but one year before the Russo-Japanese war.)

THERE ARE NO DEAD

May 13th, 1903:

"E- must be always with you."

Prayer should be always for another- for ourselves we must only pray that our sins may be forgiven and "all the rest will be added unto you. There should be prayers for those who have been called to the World Beyond- not prayers for rest, but prayers that they may be strengthened for the fulfilling of God's most Holy Will. Our Savior told us to 'pray for all men,' and man's mistake lies in thinking those who have passed from this world cannot be helped by prayer."

(In thinking of the suggestion that the name of a certain Branch of God's Church should be changed, I am told:)

"One day the whole Church of Christ will be Catholic- and the sooner that comes the better for all the world"- (from P. B.)

(I understand this as a grand unity of the Church- when "there shall be one Fold and one Shepherd.")

"The time may not be ripe for the change as yet, but the whole Church must he Catholic and Universal"- (V. B.)

May 24th, 1903:

"From this time forth the matter of the play of 'Ivan' has passed out of your hands, and out of those of Mansfield as well."

May 27th, 1903:

"Russia must pass through a severe crisis, but she will

attain to great power and glory afterwards"- (Still one year before the Russo-Japanese war.)

June 3rd:

(Reading St. Matthew xvi, 28: "Verily I say unto you, there be some standing here which shall not taste of death till they see the Son of Man coming in His Kingdom.")

"The coming of Christ is always a Spiritual coming, and they who would see His Coming would be those who would so realize His actual coming into their lives that Spiritually they would see Him."

June 10th:

"If there were no obstacles to be overcome there would be no development of character."

June 17th:

"Angels and Spirits are of totally different natures. Angels come to this world for special missions only- that is, they incarnate for special missions only- otherwise they are about us ever."

Q. "What is the meaning of the words; 'For their worm shall not die, neither shall their fire be quenched?'- (Isaiah Ixvi, 24")

A. "So long as they remain in their transgression shall this be so; but once they turn to the Lord all that must pass- the worm and the fire indicate the pangs of conscience and the fire of remorse."

August 17th:

THERE ARE NO DEAD

We see the Higher Angels only as they pass bound upon their Holy Missions- each one is like a most beautiful star. They never stop when bound upon the fulfillment of Our Lord's commands. Our Lord, Himself, is always with us; but the Higher Angels only in passing. Yes, Angels are here with us always- they are beautiful personages.

"True charity is to see the errors in yourself, but the good only in others."

"Yea, rather, being good, I came into a body undefiled"- (Wisdom of Solomon, viii, 20)- (Pythagoreans and Platonists, as well as the Jewish doctors and Rabbinical writers believed that the souls of men pre-existed and descended into suitable bodies.)

October 14th, 1903:

(Went today to see a Mrs. Stevens; a medium whom I had seen twice before, and the only one I have ever seen- and after talking for some time about "work" I would have to do, she said: "There is a chief here" (her control was an Indian) "who wants to tell you- your Father- he is a little anxious about Mary" (my Mother) "you know who it is- Mary."

At that time my Mother was perfectly well, but on October 27th, thirteen days later, she was taken from this world after a three to four days' illness of pneumonia.

October 28th:

(I am told:) "Life is not a 'troubled sleep,' but a God-given opportunity for developing the powers of the Spirit and of the Soul."

January 14th, 1904:

41

THERE ARE NO DEAD

"It is a mistaken idea that one should not give to Charity because of owing money, because one owes first and foremost to God." (This was on reading an article stating that people had no right to give to charity until all their debts were paid.)

"The second coming of Our Lord is always a Spiritual coming."

Washington, May, 1904:

(Reading of Russo-Japanese war)- "The Russian troops must fall back to Harbin" (now this was soon after the beginning of the war when such a thing appeared impossible- yet it was exactly fulfilled.)

May 22nd: "As there is no 'time' here so (also) is there no 'distance'- 'time' and 'space' do not exist here. The Spirit of God is everywhere, therefore, whatever we are doing we see you all the time."

Between Christmas and New Year, 1904-1905, I left the United States once more for a stay of a little less than two years in Russia, and from that time on have kept no regular account of things told me, only setting down special teachings, or communications from those recently called from the world. A word in regard to what is said of predestination would surely be of interest- (Romans, viii, 29-30)- "The 'predestined' are those who are sent to the world for a certain purpose, and if they are selected and sent for that purpose it is because they are known to have the strength to fulfill it.

The predestined cannot fail; those who are not predestined may fail of course, but they may also attain. The predestined are those selected and sent because it is known they cannot fail. The number of the predestined is very small in comparison to that of the non-predestined. It is a great mistake to think that all are predestined. It is a degree of development to which one must attain. A predestined person is one in whom character is rooted and grounded in the Divine. " 'I am the Resurrection and the Life'" -The Resurrection- or Anastasis- is a Spiritual turning to Christ, the giving of one's life to Him in every way, (the going upward and onward), and has nothing to do with the leaving of this world. It concerns the Spirit and not the natural body, which is but a temporary tenement of Soul and Spirit. People say the body changes every seven years; but it is a little longer than that- seven years and almost another half year before every particle of the old body is destroyed; the body changes, but the Spirit changes never- it develops or it shrinks, according as one follows 'or departs from' the way of the Lord. It must either develop or shrink, that is sure and certain. It may shrink until it becomes so materialized that it is hardly recognizable as Spirit- that constitutes death- That is the only death there is. Once the Spirit returns to Christ that is the Resurrection, or as Christ, Himself, said, the Anastasis, the 'Going upward and onward.'

"Sunday is a Holy day; but so should every day be kept Holy to the Lord. What is well to do on Sunday is well to do on Monday- and what is a good thing on one day is a good thing on another day. We do not say that Sunday must not be kept Holy to the Lord, but we do say that every other day must be kept Holy as well. As to the question of one's having other occupations during the week, there is no reason why those occupations should not be made Holy to the Lord. Dishonest transactions are always evil, but all honest business can only be made more successful by asking God's blessing upon it. If people would always think of that, the business of this Country- and of every other country as well- would be carried on on a very much higher basis. As to thinking that because one is occupied one cannot keep one's mind fixed upon God, it must be a very sad business that would prevent God's being in and with you always. A book that is evil to read on Sunday is evil to read on any other day in the week. Thoughts that are evil to think upon Sunday are evil to think at any other time. Amusements that are evil on Sunday are evil at any time.

"Jesus taught men to be happy, not sad. Sunday is a day of happiness. It is a day when the people who are shut up all the week in their counting houses or shops should, after paying homage to their God, be provided with relaxation and amusement. If this is not done the men will drink, and the women will weep. By amusement, no entertainment of a low and vulgar class is, of course, for a moment to be considered; but such places of recreation should be provided as would elevate the people's minds. The Churches of to-day are not for the people- they make no provision for the poor. The rented pews are prohibitive for those who cannot afford to pay. True, there are mission chapels, entailing an exact segregation of rich and poor. Rich and poor do not worship God in common. Make Sunday a day of joy and not of sadness. Believe that Christ came to save all men- not alone the rich. Teach men to so rule their lives that every moment is sacred to the Lord. Give up the idea appertaining to a perverted generation, namely; that Sunday is a day upon which one must serve God, while all the rest of the week one is free to follow one's earthly business in the conducting of which God has no part. Such religion is worse than none, because it only makes hypocrites of people. A man who will go to church on Sunday and confess himself a sinner, and then return to his sin (whatever it may be) for the rest of the week is surely one to be despised. Put God in all your work. Trust in Him for every breath you draw. Never let your thoughts wander from Him- or, the moment you perceive they are so doing, stop them- bring them back, and the result will be an illuminating of your whole existence. In serving God man needs no rest. Every moment should be dedicated to His service."

March 17th, 1907:

(I find here a line which is of interest.)

"K. F. tells you that you have not even begun the writing you have to do before leaving this country. That writing is going on in a way (however)- that is, you are writing little pieces that you have to put together before you can have them published- only then are they to be published. The mind awakening from sleep, or the Spirit returning to its earthly tenement, is frequently entrusted with clear messages to bring with it to people in this world. Sleep is a greatly misunderstood act of nature. A person when asleep, is absent in Spirit from the physical body- he has gone to be with other Spirits- to refresh himself for the coming day in the society of those who can teach him of Spiritual things. A very strong reason for incorrect, or disturbing dreams is to allow oneself to go to sleep with unkind thoughts of others in the heart. Nothing so disturbs one's sleep as that. A Spiritual uplift just before retiring to rest will do more to avoid distressing dreams than any other thing we can think of."

"To us, on this Plane, the ignorance of people in the world concerning Spiritual things appears unpardonable. With all the opportunities they have had of learning of the life upon this Plane, they are the most backward in knowledge concerning it of any people throughout the entire universe. A Spirit, wishing to communicate with another, goes in person to do so. The Spirit is not confined to its earthly inhabitation, even while a dweller in the world. Telepathy is a Spiritual message- or a message delivered by one Spirit to another."

Bethesda, Md., 1908:
"The body stands third in order in the organism of a

THERE ARE NO DEAD

Spiritual being. First is the Soul, which is the Breath of God-which is God. Second is the Spirit- the Ego- the man himself. Third comes the body working under the direction of Soul and Spirit. Jesus Christ is the Expression of God to the Universe.

Later- Our Lord and Savior, Jesus Christ, is the Human Expression of God. 'It is sown a natural, it is raised a Spiritual body' (1 Cor. 44). The sowing is the birth into this world, at which time the natural body is sown, or planted here for the development of its Spiritual tenant, and it is 'raised a Spiritual body' when the natural body, having fulfilled its task, is dropped, or cast aside; while the Spiritual body passes onward and upward to that plane to which it has attained, and where it must continue to fit itself for higher spheres. Birth brings us into this world. Birth takes us to the Plane beyond. Passing into a new environment is Birth."

(Q. "Why is one man cast down and another lifted up?")

A. "He who is lifted up to a pinnacle of worldly prosperity is set in the midst of many and great temptations, and may fall from grace thereby. He who is afflicted by the Lord will often turn to the Lord in his trouble. God drives a man from His Presence by prosperity, and often turns him to Himself through pain and suffering. The body lives on through change-the Spirit through development. As a Spirit develops, it passes on to higher and ever higher Planes. Man's real home is in the Spiritual world; not until man frees himself from the thought that these earthly particles must be resurrected will he cease to be earth-bound- such thoughts hold him down. Learn that Spirit only uses this fleshly covering for the short space of time it remains on this sphere, in leaving which all that is not of the Spirit is cast aside. "It is the Spirit that quickeneth the flesh profiteth nothing." (John vi, 63). The Spirit leaves all that is of the earth, and draws to itself all that is 'eternal in the Heavens,'

THERE ARE NO DEAD

Every virtue must live forever while all that Is evil must perish and fade away."

(Henry Drummond writes In the "Ascent of Man":

"The moral order is a continuous line from the beginning; it has had throughout, so to speak, a basis in the cosmos, upon which, as a trellis work, it has climbed upward to the top. The one, the trellis work, is to be conceived of as an incarnation; the other- the manifestation- as a revelation; the one is an Evolution from below, the other an Involution from above.")

(In using the phrase: "the living past," I am told:)

"There is no such thing as 'the living past'- all that was wrong In the past was destroyed- obliterated, and all that is good lives on in the present. There is the 'living present' and the 'living future'- but no such thing as the 'living past.'"

"I lay down my life that I may take it again" (John x, IT).

"I leave 'My Father's House' that I may return to it again when I shall have redeemed my people."

("Evolution is nothing but the Involution of Love, the revelation of Infinite Spirit, the Eternal Life returning to Itself."- Henry Drummond in 'The Ascent of Man.')

"Man cannot in imagination grasp the Infinite, and therefore had to be taught through the Human to attain to the Divine. 'For God giveth not the Spirit by measure unto Him- (John iii, 34). Herein lies the difference between the Son of God and humanity. The Father, the Source; the Son, the

THERE ARE NO DEAD

Transmitter; the Divine Spirit, That transmitted!"

"Spirit is the Ego- the living man- without whom the earthly body is dead; the Soul is God in man, it is what lifts man to God, Man is a living Soul."

"Through Sacrifice alone may one attain to union with the Divine."

"God made man Spirit- gave him an earthly body with which to manifest himself- and a Soul to light him to the Father! No man can love an Impersonal God. Only through Love can man come to God; therefore, through Love, did God descend into the world, taking upon Himself the form of man, in that He might bring all men unto Himself."

"Every person born into this world is watched over by his or her own especially appointed Guardian Angel. Many Angels were about Jesus during all the time He was here in the world. 'He shall give His Angels charge concerning Thee.' " (The true meaning of the temptation in Gethsemane) "It was not from His own suffering that Our Savior shrank in the Garden of Gethsemane; but, being shown by Satan, all the evil of the world, and offered by the evil spirit an opportunity of putting an immediate end to the same by His own immediate glorification as King of Israel here on this earthly plane, He had to repel this last and greatest of all the temptations in order perfectly to carry out His Heavenly Father's Will, which necessitated the suffering and Cross in order that mankind could be brought regenerate to the Father by entering into the Life of the Divine Son Whose dying to the flesh would make them capable of doing likewise. The only Spiritual Life that comes to man must come through dying to the flesh. It is self sacrifice that brings man to God- and without that Divine example this lesson could never have been learned, and man would have missed the guiding post

THERE ARE NO DEAD

to Eternal Life; would still be wandering in the wilderness without so much as a glimpse of the promised land; of the Spiritual Life to which he must attain through Christ, Our Lord, by becoming one with Him, by sharing His sufferings, by following in His footsteps, and by giving up all things for Him as He gave up His Heavenly estate to bring us to the Father."

"There is no such thing as 'going to Heaven.' You have to live in Christ, and with Christ, and that brings heaven to you, and you to heaven. Paradise is where Christ dwells- between the Eternal Father and humanity. In the World Beyond they do not sorrow over a soul that is struggling upward through many tribulations because they see the end. Life is all one Glorious Progression."

"Christ goes always into the outer darkness to seek those who are lost- but never alone- He takes one with Him through whom He may speak, a human medium whose words will reach the one He would save. They hear the Word of Life spoken by one whom Christ accompanies. Christ alone converts. The Soul of man is an infinitesimal part of God. In Jesus Christ the Soul was God. God came in person to save the world. So much of the Godhead Incarnated as was needful for the purpose of Redemption. The Spirit of God Omnipotent, Omniscient, and Omnipresent, manifested Itself through Jesus Christ, who was both God and Man. The Spirit of Christ, the Redeemer, became subject to human temptations through the Spirit of the Woman who was born of priestly race and descended from the king who was a man 'after God's own heart,' thus fulfilling God's promise to David: 'out of thee shall come a king that shall rule my people Israel.' A Spiritual Nile that should extend beyond all limitations of time forward into eternity, unto that day when all men shall be brought to God through Christ- the only Perfect Expression of God ever born into the world."

"In proportion as things that are shown to you are of help

and comfort unto others just in that proportion are they true and vital things. Son of Man- the highest type of the human- that which conjoins the human and the Divine."

(In reading the words: "For God giveth not the Spirit by measure unto Him")- "That is the only difference between the Lord and Savior, Jesus Christ, and man- the measure of the Spirit- in Him Immeasurable- in man, as he is able to receive it only. The difference is illimitable, from the lowest to the highest degree of Spiritual development, and again from the highest degree of Spiritual development as attained by man unto God- an abyss which one may cross only in Christ; He alone can lead one to God- Through Christ alone may one attain."

(Q. "What is life's purpose?")

A. "The development of the gifts of the Spirit."

(In order that the manner in which these teachings come to me may be more clearly understood, we will take now some individual cases, noting especially how each and all agree in what they have to say as to the efficacy of Intercessory Prayer, and of how greatly those in the Beyond are helped thereby.)

THERE ARE NO DEAD

CASES

I find in my journal, dated St. Petersburg, February 3rd, 1906, the following: Today K. C. came from Moscow to make me a visit. (She had been always on very friendly terms with my son, and they were about the same age.) Knowing her to be deeply interested in psychic questions, I told her of what my son had told me of rowing and swimming, and she said at once; "Do you suppose he would speak to me." After they had talked awhile, she inquired:

Q. "In what water do you swim?"

A. "In the River of Life- which gives life to all the world."

(My son then told her of their riding on horseback, and she said:)

Q. "Do you ride through space?"

A. (Somewhat indignantly) "No, we ride on the turf."

Q. "But where is it?"

A. "Here, right about you now."

Q. "But I cannot see it."

A. "Neither can we see the room in which you are, nor your earthly bodies" (K. and I were seated together on the sofa) "but (we see) your Spiritual bodies which are here with us." Very much more was said, but it was all of a personal nature and would be of no importance to others than those directly concerned. As we ceased speaking, however, I was told; "Dr. Hodgson is here and wishes to speak with you"- and another voice immediately added: "Yes, I have been here all the time and have heard all the wonderful conversation you have had this afternoon, and am perfectly overcome by it. I had no idea any such conversation could be held in that intimate way with people in the world. Of course I call it an intimate way when you can simply speak of everything you want to."

(I cannot recall whether this was the first time I had heard Dr. Hodgson speak to me after his taking from the world, but, although my impression is that it was not, I do not find anything in my notes of an earlier date. However, he has spoken to me many times since then, of which communications I shall speak later. Now we will consider some cases showing the different experiences of those who have crossed the Borderline.)

St. Petersburg, 1902:

(Reading in the paper of two young boys and two young girls who had been drowned while "crabbing" on the Lincolnshire Coast, England, I hear the words:) "We don't know at all where we are. Oh, can't you help us to find the way? It is all so dark- we can't see. We are in a field, but we can't see any light, or tell which way to go. Can't you help us? There is a young man coming toward us now- he looks like you- he can show us the way. We see that now. How strange! We did not know we had been drowned, we were fishing, and we did not know what had happened to us; but we were all in this field. Yes, all four together. And then you came to us. Yes, you were standing here beside us really; and then you brought your son to help us. He is showing us such beautiful things, and we see now we shall be so very happy here. Oh, do pray for us that we may be more happy still. No, of course we are not dead- we are very much alive- more so than we ever were before. We were so glad to see your son. We could not think what made us so happy; but now we see he has led us to the light. Oh, pray for us always- do not forget us really now.

(A day or so later, in reading some further notice of the Lincolnshire children, and praying for them, I hear at once:)-

"Oh, we are so glad you have spoken to us again. We are so very happy here in this beautiful place. We would not be in the world again for anything at all. And we are soon to have work to do; not such work as your son does, but other work that is better fitted for us, and perhaps, in time, we may come to have such work as he does now- that would be so beautiful."

October 2nd, 1902:

(Reading in the Journal de St. Petersburg of three workmen who had been run over by an express train in Austria, I hear these unhappy men beg me to help them- they have no idea where they are, but are entirely in the dark. Can see no way at all- they cannot pray, for they never did that in their lives, and do not know how.)

("Ask God to help you.")

A. "Who is God?"

(Say: " 'Our Father Who art in Heaven,' after me.")

(This they do; then I hear an exclamation, and the words:) "Now it is growing lighter, and we can see a little. Oh, don't leave us, for we don't know at all where to go, or what to do; but- there is a young man coming toward us, and it gets lighter as he comes nearer..." (From my son) "Pray for these poor men- but I can take them only a little way- yes, they can have work if they want it."

(Here they are shown a garden with flowers, and they say:) "No, we don't know anything about flowers- we only know how to work on the rails." (From my son) "I cannot show them that, but there is one here who can." (From the men) "Ah, here comes some one who we see will give us work. Yes, now we see the work we are to do; and we will not be alone, for there are some men further down the road, poor workmen like ourselves, and we can talk to them after awhile. Yes, now we are at work here, and we understand that we must work as well as we can in order to come to a lighter and brighter place."

Another case shown me in 1902 was that of a young girl whose father, at that time, occupied a prominent position in the diplomatic world, and whose mother I had known, though only slightly, when we were both young. Reading in the Paris Herald of this young girl having been called from the world, she spoke to me, saying that she was alone in a field, in darkness- then it was growing lighter, and she saw some one coming toward her, some one who was showing her the road, and she was going to a brighter place- that she had seen no one before my coming, that she did not know where she was, but did not think her father (whom she had left in the world) would be very unhappy at her going.

After some four or five days she spoke to me again, saying she had not yet found her mother (who had been taken from the world some little time before herself) but knew she should soon do so. She then repeated that I was standing just beside her, but that she also saw me "seated in a room," and then she exclaimed: "and I also see you standing beside a white marble cross with a little gold picture in it- it is in a plain with a river winding around it. What is that place?"

THERE ARE NO DEAD

(I said: "It is the place where my son's earthly body lies"- the Military Cemetery near Tiflis- and she rejoined:)

"Oh, no! that cannot be, for he is here standing just beside me, and his 'earthly body,' as you call it, is here also... he is just as much in his earthly body as I am."

("But," I objected, "you are not in your earthly body either.")

At this, she insisted with great earnestness that she had not left her earthly body, as her body was just as it always had been, only much nicer! A third time she came to tell me she had "found her mother," and was "so very happy." She said her mother did not remember having known me in the world; but when I told her my maiden name, she said her mother remembered that perfectly. She then told me she now understood what I had said about the earthly body, and knew that she had been wrong, though it had been hard for her to realize it.

A fourth time she came to beg me to tell her father about herself and her mother, that he might know how happy they both were, adding: "You will do so when you go to England, will you not?" (I have, so far, never been to England.) She then told me that she could see her father, and that she had had no idea he would be so unhappy at her going away, that it made her quite sad to see him.

St. Petersburg, 1902:

The following case is one that necessitates the relating of some personal matters, but it stands out as one of the most vivid experiences that has ever been shown me. At a wedding breakfast in St. Petersburg in the spring of 1902, I found myself seated next to the Reverend Mr. F- (a Presbyterian clergyman), then Rector of what was called the American Chapel in St. Petersburg. He had known my son, and spoke to me in very beautiful terms of his having been called so young from the world. I then told him of the gift that had been accorded me, a gift especially alluded to by St. Paul as "discerning of Spirits," I Cor. Xii:10- and of my being permitted thus to know absolutely that my son was always beside me! When I had ended, he said: "Do you know, no one ever told me such a thing as that before, and I thank you most sincerely for speaking of it."

A few days later I met Mr. F- again, and he said he had been to call upon me, and had regretted greatly not having found me at home, as he had had something most important to tell me. In brief, it was this: On the day following that of the wedding breakfast, he was sent for to see a Russian woman whose husband, a noted sculptor, had been called, a few days earlier, from this world. Mr. F- had never met this lady, and was greatly astonished at the summons, but she said that she had sent for him because she wished to tell of a thing of which she could not speak to her own people (they were a Jewish family). She then told him that, although her husband was, what the world called, "dead," he, himself, was continually beside her- looking as he had looked before his calling from the world, and guiding and counseling her in all she had to do. "She was perfectly calm- in no way excited," continued my informant, "but if it had not been for what you had just told me, I should not have understood one word of what she said."

This is but the preface to a very remarkable interview- if I may so call it- that I had a few days later. I was returning from the English Church in St. Petersburg after an early celebration of the Holy Eucharist one Sunday morning, and on the way my thoughts reverted to the story Mr. F- had told me, and I also thought of an account I had read the day before of the sudden passing from this world of a Mme. Levi (an accident) who had told me from the Beyond that she was very unhappy. Walking along and thinking of this woman, I asked: "Is it because she was a Jewess that she is so unhappy?" when suddenly I feel that the other- the sculptor- is beside me, and I hear the words: "Not in any way- I, myTself, am a Jew, and I am very happy here."

"That," I said, "is because you see your wife always." It really is impossible to give any idea of the vividness of the conversation that ensued, and in copying the notes I made at the time, they seem totally inadequate to describe it.

"Yes," he said, "I see her, and she both sees me and we talk together. I am in a beautiful spot- No! I do not believe in the Christ, Yes, I made a statue of Him. I was never taught in that way- I am a Jew." ("But He, also, was a Jew!")

"That is true; but I never learned anything about Him"- (he surely must have forgotten, as how could he have made a statue of the Savior without having studied about Him.")

("All your Prophets speak of Him.")

"Was it so?" No, I really do not know. Yes; of course, I believe in David. Yes, I pray also that God may show me the truth; but I am not unhappy. Still, I want to know the truth. There are some people coming toward me now. I have never seen anything like them since I have been here, and surely not in the world! And there is a Light something new and strange coming into my life- the Light is here beside me. Oh, do not stop praying for me, or it will go away."

(Involuntarily I made the Sign of the Cross)

"What have you done? You have made the Sign of the Cross upon my forehead- I feel it. Oh, how much brighter everything has grown, the flowers, the trees, everything- and there is a young man coming to me. He looks like you. You say it is your son? And your husband is with him, too. They will help me to understand that I see at once. Oh, this change is wonderful! Tell my wife of it for me."

("No, I cannot do that; you must do that yourself.")

"Then promise me you will go to see her, and tell her of my having spoken, and after that I can make her understand. Thank God that you have prayed for me."

(This is about one-fiftieth part of all that was said, but it is in no wise possible to inscribe it all, or to give any idea of the intense vividness with which the words came to me as I passed along the Quay and the busy streets on the way back to my own apartment. I went to see the sculptor's wife as he asked me to do, but found she had left for her country place, and I heard afterwards that she had gone from there abroad. Up to this present time I have never met her, but hope still to do so one day.)

St. Petersburg, September, 1902:

(From my note book): Today the name is given me of a friend who had been recently taken from the world, and I ask what I can do for her? She begs me to pray for her; says she is in utter darkness, and has seen no one since she went there! I do pray for her, but still she sees no light. I tell her to try to pray for herself, but she says she cannot- she does not know how- she never prayed. No, she does not remember the Lord's Prayer- she never knew it! After a little hesitation she repeats it after me, then, she tells me there are many people she does not like, and cannot think kindly of; but when I tell her it is those very thoughts that keep her from coming to the light, she promises to put them from her!

Again she begs me to pray for her as no one else does
so- "none of my children pray"- but, she says she will not forget
the Lord's Prayer. Then after we have talked a long time, she tells
me she sees a Light coming toward her, and that things are
growing less dark- "some such beautiful people; they are coming
to me, I see"- Then they are standing beside her. (I beg them to
lead her to the Light) and she says; "It has grown quite light,"
then exclaims "Oh, your husband is here, and he has brought
such a beautiful young man with him- it must be your son, he
looks so much like you. Oh, your husband will help me I know. I
was always so fond of you both, and he was always so nice to
me and to... I am sure he will help me find, I should be so happy
then. It has been so terrible seeing no one all this time. Oh, this
place is so much more beautiful! I see now that I can really be
happy here. Thank God that you prayed for me... I never thought
I should want anyone to pray for me."

St. Petersburg, September, 1903:

The next is a case that extended over a period of several
months, and I may even say years, since those who spoke to me
then are still apt at any moment to do so. You may remember
having heard of a terrible automobile accident that occurred in
France at that time, in which a Mr. and Mrs. Fair were killed. As
I read of it in the Paris Herald (in St. Petersburg) I heard Mrs.
Fair instantly speak to me. She seemed greatly astonished at
what had happened, and unable to comprehend exactly just
where she was. Later Mr. Fair spoke, and we had a long talk
together, of which I have not kept a detailed account. They (the
Fairs) said, however, that they were not very happy.

The Paris Herald of September 10th contained an
account of the funeral service held in Paris for Mr. and Mrs. Fair,

and, after reading it, I prayed for them, and at once heard the words; "Oh, thank God you have prayed for us again. No, we are not very happy, but so much happier than we were at first. We are no longer in that dark place where we could see nothing at all, but even here we cannot see very much. But now you have prayed for us, your son will come again to help us. Oh, we see him coming now. He is taking us by such a lovely road; now we see we shall be happy, and this road is so lovely we do not seem to care for anything at all. Oh, thank God for your praying for us, as it let your son come to help us once more. Oh, tell our people in the world how much it helps one here to be just and true in all one's dealings, and to make one's life of help and service to others in the world. Oh, Friend, whom we did not know in the world, pray for us always. Now we are so much happier than we thought we could ever be- thanks to the prayers you have made for us. Yes, say that, we wish you to say that. Goodbye... pray for us."

On September 15th, they tell me distinctly: "We are happy now. We have been so nervous while they were taking those poor bodies about" (their earthly remains were taken to California) "but now they have finished with that, thank God- and your son has helped us so very much."

(From my son:) "We could scarcely leave Mr. and Mrs. Fair at all while they were taking those bodies about in the boat and trains. They were so nervous for fear something would happen to them, though they, themselves, are here so bright and well."

(From the Fairs:) "And so thankful for all that has been given us now. Do not forget to tell our people of all this- for Christ's sake."

THERE ARE NO DEAD

September 30th:

In reading, in the Herald of the final interment of Mr. and Mrs. Fair, they say: "Thank God you have prayed for us again, for now we know help will come. Yes, we are not so unhappy; but we cannot seem to get along alone at all. Now we know your son will come to help us; he must be coming now, for we see some one so tall and- light- now he is taking us by this beautiful road, it is perfectly lovely. It is so strange we cannot find it alone, for it is so clear and straight. You must not forget to write to us often."

Mr. and Mrs. Fair have spoken to me many times since, and always ask me to speak to their friends of this. As I have had, however, no occasion of meeting their friends, they beg that I will mention them by name in hopes that the message will thus reach those for whom it is destined. The last case that I shall relate is one of a different character, and I am not at liberty to disclose the names of the people concerned therein:

Hearing one day in April, 1911, of the sudden taking from this world of a lady who was cousin to very dear friends of mine, and with whom I, myself, was but slightly acquainted, I, upon re-entering my own room, felt myself suddenly impelled to pray for her. Hardly had I done so when, to my astonishment, came the words: "Pray for..." (giving me the name of her cousin, and one of my dear friends).

(Q. "Why do you ask that?")

A. "That she may not come to the lonely place where I am.""

(I then asked her to pray in the Name of Our Lord and Savior, Jesus Christ, but she said that she heard me say to pray in

61

A Name, but she could not hear the Name. She knew if she could hear It, she could be taken to the Father—, but she could not hear it at all; and yet she knew until she did hear it, she could not be where she would be happy.)

(Praying with all my strength that help might he shown her, a voice answered:) "She is with the dead- for she is dead."

("But," I exclaimed, "there are no dead!")

And the answer came: "None save those who do not believe in the Name of Our Lord and Savior, Jesus Christ, Who is the Resurrection and the Life, and if they do not believe in Him they have no life in them, and will never be happy until they come to Him. Those who have rejected Him in this World lose His Name upon passing to the World Beyond, and eons may pass before they are privileged to hear It again."

All this startled me greatly, for I knew the woman who had crossed the Border-line to be one given to many good works, and so, when she asked me to write to her cousin of this I simply could not do it. Furthermore, as I expected to see my friends during the summer months, I thought it would be easier to speak than to write upon the subject. No opportunity, however, presented itself for so doing, and finally, one August morning, I was told I must write out exactly what had been told me and give it to... asking her to read it carefully when she was alone, and after reading it, to pronounce aloud the Name that she (the one in the Beyond) had forgotten, as in that way alone could she hear and know it again. Now, both of these friends of mine- the one who crossed the Border-line, and the one in this world- were Unitarians, and I had no idea as to how the latter would receive the message; but, reflecting that that was not the part with which I had to do, I, after writing it out as I had been directed, gave it to my friend as she was about starting on a two days' automobile

THERE ARE NO DEAD

trip.

It was on the morning after her return from this long ride that, as I passed the house, my friend called me, and as we stood there in the brilliant sunlight, she told me that she had read the paper as soon as she had gone to her room, and that she had immediately pronounced The Name aloud- and had felt, as she did so, that her cousin stood beside her, and that all was well. "But, after this, for two entire days," continued my friend, "I could do nothing but repeat The Name over and over to myself; and always I could feel her happiness as I did so."

Before this, however, on the afternoon of the day on which I had delivered the paper, I had heard from the one in the Beyond that she had "heard The Name that she had forgotten, and knew It as the Name of Him Who alone could bring her to the Father; that she believed, through the word that... had spoken, in the Lord and Savior, Jesus Christ!"

Amazed that so dread a thing could happen to a woman so thoughtful of others as had been the one in question, I besought enlightenment, and was told:

"It was just because she was a woman very spiritually developed that she was able to grasp the stupendous fact that something of vital import was missing in her life."

Extract from a Letter from Dr. Hodgson, March 15th, 1901:

Dear Mrs. de Meissner:

Yours of March 13th to hand... As regards your experiences in connection with the appearance of Christ after the Resurrection, I think, myself, there can be little doubt that

THERE ARE NO DEAD

Chirst's body was not exactly a flesh and blood body like ours. I believe that this question has been discussed a great deal by various theologians, some of whom have taken, I think, quite rightly, the view that it was Christ's Spiritual body, but that the eyes of His disciples were opened to perceive it. There are, of course, difficulties in any interpretation.

The appearance and disappearance of the body would be in favor of this view; on the other hand, the incident related in connection with Thomas. Continued aspiration and prayer to the Highest are necessary always to get the best that is possible for us in the way of communication from the other side.

Yours sincerely, R. Hodgson.

The above letter was one written in answer to a "communication" that had been given me concerning the Resurrection of Our Lord, and of which I had written to Dr. Hodgson. It was after hearing a sermon in which St. Paul's words: "Sown a natural body, it is raised a spiritual body" were quoted, that the thought had crossed my mind: "Why then did Our Lord appear in His natural body?" And I was told:

"Because it is not given to mortal eye to behold Spiritual form, therefore Our Lord was obliged to make use of His natural body in order that He might be seen of the many who were to testify to the Resurrection."- (I Cor. XV : 6.)

("Did this same natural body ascend to Heaven- and how.")

"It did, because having served as the Temple of the Incarnate God It had, Itself, become wholly Spiritualized."

THERE ARE NO DEAD

American Branch of the Society for Psychical Research Boston, Mass., March 28th, 1901:

Dear Mrs. de Meissner:

Thank you very much for the account of your extremely interesting experience. We shall be glad to get any additional statement, should it be possible, from other persons concerned. If, for example, your husband's cousin could give us some account of your desire not to go out on the evening of April 16th, 1896, her statement will be valuable. It is, of course, not surprising that all the statements made to you have not been absolutely correct. You must remember always that so long as you retain consciousness, the communications that come to you from your departed friends are sure to be affected, to some extent, by yourself. They will either be affected by the machine of your organism so to speak, or else they will be affected by coming through your subliminal self, and there is always a liability to some change in the original communication owing to this fact. Very frequently as I believe mistakes or confusions in communications are often quite erroneously attributed to the spirits themselves, yet they should be really attributed to the incarnate individualities through whom the messages come.

We shall be always glad to hear from you of your further experiences.

Yours sincerely, R. Hodgson.

Boston, Mass., March 30th, 1901:

Dear Mrs, de Meissner:

Thank you for your further kind letter of March 28th... Of course I agree with what you half suggest, that it is not

65

desirable for us to try and lift the veil as regards our individual futures; but our friends on the other side do sometimes think wise to give us occasionally some indications.

Yours sincerely, R. Hodgson.

November 7th, 1901:

(This letter refers to communication from Captain E- in which the word congenial is used.)

I did not intend in my previous letter to suggest that the remark of your friend in connection with the word "congenial" seemed in any way unnatural. It carried with it, in fact, an intrinsic touch of strong realism.

Yours sincerely, R. Hodgson.

November 28th, 1902:

Dear Mrs. de Meissner:

In reply to yours of November 25th, I shall be glad to see every word that you get that seems to come from Myers. There is a fundamental truth in the statement that "they try to impose conditions on the spirits instead of bringing themselves to the point where we can meet them," and of course our friends on the other side can be helped by prayer just as much as ourselves.

Yours sincerely, R. Hodgson.

(The words in quotation marks were what had been told me from the Beyond concerning the manner in which attempts are usually made upon this plane to communicate with those in the Spiritual World.)

THERE ARE NO DEAD

December 20th, 1902.:

Did you know either Mr. or Mrs Fair personally? I have no doubt myself that our friends on the other side can be helped by us, both by prayer and advice, if we are in such relations with them as to be able to give it to them. I shall be glad always to receive any accounts of any communications which you receive from any persons.

Yours sincerely, R. Hodgson.

January 7th, 1903:

Dear Mrs. de Meissner:

Thank you very much for yours of January 1st to hand, together with your articles on prayer and death. I think I agree with everything you say there I send you a Christmas card which is late for Christmas, but I hope that the quotation may give you pleasure.

Yours sincerely, R. Hodgson.

"The Ghost in Man, the Ghost that once was Man,
But cannot wholly free itself from Man,
Are calling to each other thro' a dawn
Stranger than earth has ever seen; the veil

Is rending, and the Voices of the day
Are heard across the Voices of the dark.
No sudden heaven, nor sudden hell, for man.
But thro' the Will of One who knows and rules

And utter knowledge is but utter love
Aeonian Evolution, swift or slow.

THERE ARE NO DEAD

Thro' all the spheres- an ever opening height.
An ever lessening earth."

Tennyson.

November 28th, 1903:

Thank you very much for your kind letter of November 18th. The experience in connection with S- passing over is striking, and is in line with what I believe to be generally the case, that our friends on the other side are aware when some one specially near is about to pass over. The prayer is very beautiful.

Yours sincerely, R. Hodgson.

(The experience to which Dr. Hodgson here alludes was one that happened to me during the night preceding my Mother's taking from the world. She had been ill for two days, but we had not known until the previous evening that she was suffering from pneumonia. A trained nurse had then been immediately called, but we still had no idea of there being any immediate danger. At eleven P.M. I went into the room adjoining my Mother's, leaving the door open between the two, and requesting the nurse to call me if any change occurred.

I was very tired and fell into a deep sleep, from which I was suddenly roused by hearing my name called in loud, authoritative tones. Confused and bewildered, I sat up, wondering who had called me, and for what? Suddenly I realized that it was my husband's voice, and at the same time I heard him say aloud: "Go in to your Mother quickly- she is lonely." Hurrying to her bedside I found my mother moving restlessly, as though she were looking for some one, and the nurse told me she had just awakened and appeared very agitated. As soon as I seated myself by her bed and took both her hands in mine, she

THERE ARE NO DEAD

became quiet, and dropped off again to sleep. That was at two A.M., and we had no idea of her being in any danger at that time, but six hours later she passed suddenly to the Grander Life Beyond.

The prayer to which Dr. Hodgson refers in the above letter is the one on the first page of this book.)

15 Charles St., December 28th, 1903:

Dear Mrs. de Meissner:

I was very much pleased to receive your kind letter of December 26th. Your experience with your departed friends is a very interesting one, and I have known cases even at the Piper trances where a communicator seemed in doubt for a short time whether the sitter was discarnate or incarnate. Truly, indeed, our prayers can help the departed. I am reminded of a little poem by Henry Ames Blood, which I shall have some type copies made of, and send you one. If you haven't seen it, I'm sure it will please you. With best wishes for your happiness and growing "light" this coming year,

I am, sincerely, Richard Hodgson.

A PRAYER

For the dead and for the dying,
For the dead that once were living,
And the living that are dying.
Pray I to the All-forgiving.
For the dead who yester journeyed,
For the living, who, to-morrow.
Through the Valley of the Shadow,
Must all bear the world's great sorrow;

THERE ARE NO DEAD

For the immortal, who, in silence,
Have already crossed the portal;
For the mortal, who, in sadness,
Soon shall follow the immortal.
Keep thine arms round all, O Father!
Round lamenting and lamented;
Round the living and repenting,
Round the dead who have repented.
Keep thine arms round all, O Father!
That are left or that are taken;
For they all are needy, whether
The forsaking or forsaken.

Henry Ames Blood.

(I do not recall exactly what I wrote at the time to Dr. Hodgson about this poem, except that I said I did not care for the term "The Valley of the Shadow," but my letter brought the following in reply :)

January 10th, 1904:

Dear Mrs. de Meissner:

For my own part I shall look forward with great rejoicing to "Death," and you and various other people may also. But those who do are comparatively few. Even most of those whose lives are comparatively miserable have a shrinking from "Death." This is the fact. For most people it is a "Valley of the Shadow," and for most people there is a time of sadness for them in the contemplation of it. That if they were wiser, if they knew more- they would not have any sadness or shadow- makes no difference to their need, I should say. Of course the verses would have been still better if they recognized the other aspect also, and included those who waited the transition in joy.

THERE ARE NO DEAD

Richard Hodgson.

November 10th, 1904:

Dear Mrs. de Meissner:

In reply to your kind letter of November 5th, sending me another copy of "The Higher Life," I received a previous copy in the summer and read it with pleasure. I should have written to thank you for it. There must be an enormous number of persons to whom it would prove of great help and consolation. In fact, anyone who is conscious of the spiritual nature at all should be strengthened by it. I wish you could tell me of the communications which you had more than two and a half years ago in St. Petersburg, and which, apparently, have relation to the present war in the East. I will keep them absolutely private. What address do you wish to be given for the receipt of your future Journals and Proceedings? Shall they be sent to Washington, D.C, or do you wish to give some St. Petersburg address?

Yours sincerely, R. Hodgson.

"The Higher Life," of which Dr. Hodgson here speaks, was a booklet I published at that time telling of the manner in which this power of communicating with those in the Beyond had first come to me, and of the wonderful help and comfort it had proved. It was sold in aid of the Red Cross work in the Far East. The communications, or a part of them, concerning the Russo-Japanese war have already been inserted in these papers. The following letter is not of any special importance except because of its being the last letter I received from Dr. Hodgson, as I left for Russia the latter part of the month of December, 1904, and Dr. Hodgson was taken from this world during the ensuing year:

THERE ARE NO DEAD

December 17th, 1904:

Dear Madame de Meissner:

In reply to yours of December 14th Thank you for further information concerning Count Keller. I shall be glad if you will send me any future prophecies concerning persons, or incidents, in connection with the war immediately you receive them, and before fulfillment. I think it will be kind if you would send a copy of "The Higher Life" to the head office in London. We are having your address changed at this office, and also sending notification of change to England. Should you stop in London on your return to this country, you can call at the office of the S. P. R. there, which is 20 Hanover Square, and ascertain when any meetings will be held. Probably you will know beforehand by looking at your Journal. You will have a right, of course, to attend any meetings that may be held by virtue of your membership in the American Branch. With kindest regards always.

Yours sincerely, R. Hodgson.

Dr. Hodgson's words in regard to Count Keller relate to a very vivid message I had received the previous summer concerning that distinguished officer, who had relinquished his post as Commandant of the Corps of Imperial Pages in St. Petersburg to take part in the war in the East. On July 26th, 1901, in reading of battles in which Generals Rennenkampf and Keller were engaged, I was told that, "the first would be most successful in harassing the Japanese with his Cossacks throughout the entire war"; and when I asked: "What of the second?" I was told: "He will be taken from the world in a few days."

Taking up the Washington Post of August 2nd, 1904, at

THERE ARE NO DEAD

Atlantic City, where I then was, I read in large headlines; "Count Keller dead," and found that that gallant officer had been mortally wounded while directing the fire from a battery on July 31st. What was told me in regard to General Rennenkampf was also absolutely fulfilled, although that of course could not have been seen until after Dr. Hodgson had been taken from the world.

I find inscribed under date of St. Petersburg, November 2nd, 1905, the following: This morning at five o'clock heard Conrad speak (the son of a dear friend of mine. He was a few months older than my son, and passed to the Higher Life six months after my son had done so) and he had so much to say about the beautiful library/ where were books such as were never dreamed of in this world, and which he could take out and keep as long as he liked. No two people ever wished to study up a subject at the same time, and he would lie on the grass under the big trees and read- and each time he finished a book he found it to be the subject he needed for the instruction of the next person he had to meet on their arrival in the World Beyond. He was not distinctly told which book to take, but it always proved to be the one he needed. He told me that S (my son) did not read as much as he, but said he seemed to know all about the instruction he had to give, and that he met every soldier and officer who came to the World Beyond from the war in the East.

He was there to instruct them in all they had to do- both officers and men- and that he was in the camp every day and saw to all the arrangements. To give out to the world any communication as coming from Doctor Hodgson at once opens wide the door to criticism, though why one so deeply interested in the study of the relations between the seen and the unseen as was the late Secretary of the American Branch of the S. P. R. should refrain from communicating from the Beyond did he find a way open for so doing, it is difficult to state. Or why, having communicated through others, he should fail to speak to one with whom he had corresponded for some four or five years it is also difficult to understand. Therefore, without further preface I shall simply give the ensuing communications as I find them jotted down in my note book under the dates mentioned, believing them myself to be from Doctor Richard Hodgson.

St. Petersburg, February 21, 1906:

"There is a very important thing Dr. Hodgson wishes you to say for the enlightenment of those who are interested in the study of the wonderful question of the relations between this world and the world to come, and it is this; 'I want you to move over there to where the picture of Our Lord and Savior, Jesus Christ, is. Now I can write better. To begin with, I want people to understand that by His Name alone can they be saved—that there is no other name in all the world by which they can be saved. I have learned this only since I have been here. I had thought that a profound knowledge of the experiences of the existence here was all that was necessary for a thorough enjoyment of the future life- as we speak of it in the world- but I find that that is not in any way the case. I found upon coming here that I was not prepared in any way for the conditions of this life; for the fact of there being nothing in the world to prepare one for this life other than a complete knowledge of the work and of the Life of Our Lord and Savior, Jesus Christ, and I beseech those who are interested in the study of the Life to come to adopt that study in preference to the scientific methods they now employ.

I know perfectly well that they will say there are no proofs in that method of study, but that is entirely false. Every proof can be had if it is sought for according to the Life of Our Lord and Savior, Jesus Christ. That is all I can say today- but I have more to add at another time.

THERE ARE NO DEAD

Yes, I want you to help me now to convey to the world all the things that are being taught to me here- that is exactly what I said- that they would have proofs through the Life of Our Lord and Savior, Jesus Christ- and in time it will be given me to make them clear to them. No, that is not all. I want to answer the question that came into your mind- No! I have not seen Mr. Myers yet; but I know that I have to see him, shortly, and at that time you can be of great help to me."

(Q. "How so.?")

A. "By praying for me that I may see Mr. Myers- now- at once. Yes, I see Mr. Myers coming now toward me, and I am so glad and happy. I can hardly thank God enough for what He has allowed you to do for me. Now Mr. Myers is taking me along a road I had supposed I had to follow, but I did not know it surely until he came. We are both most deeply thankful to have found one another, and we pray Our Father to let you pray for us in order that we may understand and help you in all the work you have to do in the world"

(Here followed some further remarks about the work I should have to do, and with those the conversation ended.)

February 22nd, 1906:

"In the first place Doctor Hodgson wishes you to say for him today that he knows perfectly well all the difficulties there will be in showing to people the beautiful things of this life- where everything is on so beautiful a scale- and where everything is so exactly similar to what is in the world that it is exceedingly difficult to describe the difference."

(Q. "What was your impression upon arriving there?")

THERE ARE NO DEAD

A. "You must tell them first that I had no idea at all (that) I had left the world, but simply found myself lying upon a sofa in a room I did not quite recognize. Then I got up and went out of the house and found a friend whom I had known in the world, and he took me to a certain place where I had to stay for several days. I cannot tell you anything about those days because I cannot exactly remember all about them; but I know I was not exactly happy because I had no idea of where I was. I did not find any other friend at all. No, it was as though I were in a desert place after the friend went away. No, it was not strange- I know now that it was as though I were put there in order to accustom myself to the changed conditions of existence, that is, to the greater rarification of the atmosphere, and then also, I had to learn that I was no longer under the same conditions of living as in the world. I understood at that time that I had passed to the Higher Life, and that was what I had not understood at first.

It (this knowledge) came first through the prayer that you offered up for me. I had understood nothing until that time. It was because I was so taken up with the scientific view of the question that I had entirely neglected the Spiritual side. I see exactly what you think- that people will think you are writing this in order to draw them to Christ- but you cannot draw them except by what I can show you now- that is, that you must explain to them exactly what is told to you by those in the World Beyond, and those who are destined to believe will at once do so, while others will not believe any more than if they had never heard the message.

It is a case of Faith- only those who have Faith can learn of this- because of their unbelief they cannot be shown, any more than could those be healed who would not believe in the power of Our Lord and Savior, Jesus Christ, to heal them. That is all I have to say today, but Mr. Myers has a word to say to you."

THERE ARE NO DEAD

(From Mr. Myers) "I thank you very much, my friend, for praying for me, and now I want to tell you this: It is that I am very happy indeed to find that I can continue my work from this plane of Life, and that it does not depend at all on our being in the world, the power of carrying out our work"- (here followed a good deal about changes he would wish made in his book, then:)- "I will begin at the very commencement of my life here, which is, after all, but a gradual uplifting to a higher sphere where all the conditions of life are exactly as they are upon the earth, only increased a thousandfold in Spirituality. I knew very much of that before I came here because I felt always that it was the Spiritual life alone that was of consequence. As my friend. Doctor Hodgson, told you.

When you tell people about these things I would not have them think that it is I alone who tell you this- there are many others who tell you the same thing. Your own son is beside you always."

(Q. "How do you know?")

A. "I see him beside you always. I can describe him if you wish. I think I had better tell you that I see him exactly as you saw him in the world."

(Q. "Through my mind?")

A. "No, not through your mind at all, but tall, and straight, and handsome- beside you."

(Q. "An Angelic apparition?")

A. "No. How can you think of such a thing? I see him in his military uniform, just as he always was when in the world"- (In Russia the officers never wear civilian dress.)

"And now I want to tell you one more thing. I want you to write this book- yes, 'this book'- (here there is some little confusion, as I do not understand to what book Mr. Myers refers, and he closes with the remark: "Doctor Hodgson and I are aiding you to write a book.")

February 23rd, 1906:

(From Dr. Hodgson): "There is one thing we want you very much to say, and that is that there is a life beyond the grave- as people say- though in reality that is not a correct expression since we never see the grave, but are led by Divine Omnipotence directly here, so that upon awakening we find ourselves in an atmosphere of love and tender care for us which we are not accustomed to in the world. Yes, many of us are not accustomed to that- go and shut the window, you will take cold- we want others to know that there is no separation at all, that we are always with those we love and who think of us, as their thoughts attract us there to where they are, and we feel and think with them always.

I do not think that I can say any more for the moment, but I know that Mr. Myers wishes very much to speak with you today."

(From Mr. Myers). "Yes, Mr. Myers, of the S. P. R.- I have this to tell you, Mme. De Meissner, for my friend, Doctor Hodgson, has told me who you are, that I feel that I am going to be able to carry on my work very completely now- there was so very much that I did not finish that I feel that it has to be done at once..."

March 2nd, 1906:

"It is Doctor Hodgson who wishes to speak to you

today... There are many ways of being saved, but there is but One Name by which it may be brought about, and that is the Name of Our Lord and Savior, Jesus Christ- Doctor Hodgson especially wishes to say this because he knows perfectly well that the people in the world think that there is another way, or many ways, by which they may be saved- but on coming here that is the first thing that is shown to one; not that it is shown to all at once, because there are many who do not know of that until after many years (as we count them here) of suffering."

(Q. "Of suffering?")

A. "Yes, of suffering! Because the suffering of this world is a thing that must be counted with. It is a thing which no one can escape who does not believe in the Name of Our Lord and Savior, Jesus Christ! That Name will save many, even of those who have not led the lives in the world that they should have led, and yet have believed in the Mercy of Our Lord and Savior, Jesus Christ.

Yes, I know perfectly well what you think- to whom much is given (of him) will much be required- and that is surely so. And yet, I know that although I did not believe it was essential to Salvation to believe in the Divinity of Our Lord and Savior, Jesus Christ, I also am aware of the fact that I would never have known as much as I now know had I not thought it possible that He might be God and the son of God; and therefore I was allowed to understand this at once, and to know that in that way alone may one be brought to repentance and obtain forgiveness of their sins. Now it is Mr. Myers who wants to speak to you again."

(From Mr. Myers)... "Yes, I found the ideas expressed in the book ('Human Personality') in great part correct. The conditions of life here are just about what I thought. One undergoes no change of personality in any way at all. One sees only that everything is of a very much higher order of existence, but in the actual conditions of life there is no change whatsoever. Yes, the pursuits with which one occupied one's self in the world are the ones with which one continues to occupy one's self here, except in cases where those pursuits were distasteful in the world; in such cases the occupation most in accordance with one's own personal inclinations are given one.

Everyone is not occupied at once. Many do not understand that that is the highest form of perfecting one's self- that only in that way may one advance in everything that is beautiful in the way of knowledge. There are lectures- there are literary pursuits of every kind! In regard to those demonstrations of the continuity of Life as given in the S. P. R. they are of the very lowest order and cannot make any real impression on high-souled people of the world who look for something infinitely more spiritual than a mere perception of a poor wandering Spirit who has no hope of attaining to any comprehension of the state of existence accorded to those believing in the Name of Our Lord and Savior Jesus Christ for many eons to come. There, I cannot say any more today. I thank our Father for letting me show you this- later I can show you much more on this subject. It is most interesting and beautiful, and I thank our Father for having let me show you this... It is from Frederic Meyers- yes, that is right."

(From Mr. Myers). "My ideas were, only very crude ideas of the Divine Truths that have now been shown me."

Bethesda, Md., June 15th, 1909:

Doctor Hodgson, speaking of his having told me he "saw himself in the glass just as he always had been- (I do not find the record of that communication, but at the time of receiving it I sent a copy to Doctor Hyslop in New York)- said: "I see myself less often now in the glass than I did, we seem to need those things less as time goes on. I want you to write to Doctor Hyslop and tell him conditions change. I told you I saw myself in the glass on making my toilet- that was at first- now there is a change; I don't seem to need the earthly things I did at first. Our life runs along on other lines- (You are not a very good medium, but I can tell him some things through you I cannot tell him through another, now wait a moment, go on with what I was saying- that is:)- it seems (our life) to move away from the needs of earth, and we find our Spiritual needs of more moment. We want to help the Society (S. P. R.) but we have to do it in our own way."- (here followed some messages for Doctor Hyslop concerning communications he had received through different mediums which I did not understand but transmitted as requested. I should here state that copies of all of Doctor Hodgson's letters given in this book, as well as of many others not given, were made by Doctor Hyslop for preservation in the archives of the American Society of Psychical Research.)

Here we will close this little record which aims only at showing, first- the conditions governing the life on the plane succeeding this in so far as they have been made clear to me; and second- the immense help that may be afforded those who have been taken from this world by a loving, heart-felt prayer! Do not think of your child whom God has called to a higher plane of existence as being in some far off distant star, or planet. The world's visible and invisible inter-penetrate. There is no separation anywhere. Those who profess to love their own who have been taken from this world yet appear to shrink in terror if it be suggested that their beloved ones are still beside them. In other words they would seem to care only for the material body, the gross earthly covering, and not at all for the beautiful Spirit who has been its tenant, and who still stands beside them, clothed in that Spiritual body which alone is "eternal in the heavens"; the "house not made with hands" of which St. Paul tells us (H Cor. V, 1). No, man is not made to die! We have eternal life in Jesus Christ. This eternal life is our heritage in Him. No man can take it from us. The mistake is to look upon this eternal life as something extraneous to ourselves; something we shall enter into when we leave this earthly body, whereas, all Life is one; Eternity is of the past as of the future: "And this is the record, that God hath given to us Eternal Life, and this Life is in His Son." (I John, V, 11.)

Hardly had these last lines been written than was received the report of the disaster to the White Star liner, "Titanic." This occurred on the night of Sunday, April 14th, and on Wednesday, April 17th, as I was wondering whether William T. Stead, with whom I had frequently corresponded, had indeed been lost, I received the following communication from him: "I cannot understand why everyone is so depressed because of that- (the disaster)- I am very happy, and would not be in the world again for anything." Meeting, on April 18th, a friend who receives from time to time strong psychic impressions, and who was personally acquainted with Major Archibald Butt, I was told by her that Major Butt had given her to understand that he was most anxious to send a message to Washington. When she inquired, however, as to whether he could not give it to her, he replied: "No, but you have a friend who could take it for me."

Nothing more was said upon the subject, but an hour or so later, I, being at that time down town shopping, was suddenly aware of the fact that Major Butt was trying to speak to me, and as I protested inwardly: "I can never listen to you here," the words "I will speak with you later," were given slowly and distinctly. That evening I went from the dinner table directly to my room- it was then about eight o'clock- firmly impressed with the idea there would be a message for me from Mr. Stead. When I had asked whether there was anything he wished to say, I received the following:

"I simply went from my cabin directly to the Beyond. I never suffered at all. I did not even know where I was until I saw Julia."- (those who have read Mr. Stead's book, "Letters from Julia," will understand)- "she was there to welcome me..."

("And your son?" I inquired.)

"And my son, of course. I never knew Julia very well in the world, but we are fast friends now; and as to my son, if you could only believe it- I will tell you I am so happy I can hardly contain my joy- the boy is here, and we are together once more."

("You understand?" I ventured.)

"I have understood always- thank God!"

Immediately after these words I felt that another person stood beside me, and upon asking who it was received the reply; "It is Archie Butt, of course." (April 18th- 8:30 P.M.) Then came the following: "I have wanted so much to speak to some one in the world. I want to get a message through to the President- I mean Mr. Taft- Will you give it to him for me?"

(I ask in the Name of our Lord and Savior, Jesus Christ, whether I may do so, and Major Butt adds :)

"It is in His Name alone I would ask you to do it."

("But how can I?")

"You will give him the message as I give it to you, that is all. Tell the President- the friend whom I do not know will tell him that I have never felt more entirely and unutterably happy than I do at this very moment. Every care I ever had has slipped away. I feel only so glad and thankful I could do a little to help all those who were so terrified, and I only wish I could have done more. Now I beg that no one will mourn in any way because I am no longer in the world. I never cared so greatly for all the things I was supposed to care for- but I do care to have left the President at this moment. I might have been of service to him, yet surely, if I am here, it is all for the best.

He will find someone else who can be of service to him, and I am so thankful everything is over- and I find myself alive, intensely alive; so much so that I cannot see the slightest difference in my own appearance or feel any difference in my own feelings- if I may so express myself- between now and the time of my being in the world. It is certainly most strange! There is one thing I would say to the President to make him know this is from Archie Butt...

I wished to speak to you, and I knew, because Mr. Stead told me that he could speak to you, that I could do it also. No, you did not know Mr. Stead personally though you had corresponded with him- and so, when I said I wanted to write to some one in Washington, he told me of your being there, and I found a friend of yours first, and she spoke to you about me and that is why you prayed for me, and that brought me to where you were, and so I was able to speak to you. You will only need to give him the message, and you won't need to say anything more. No- not for the moment- wait till you hear from the ship, and don't fail then to send this at once, saying it was given you at this date (April 18th, 1912, 9:30 P.M.) but that you had heard me speak to you a few hours earlier also (4 P.M. of the same day). Tell President Taft I want him not to be sad or disheartened at my being taken from the world, for I have never known such happiness as I now feel in all the existence in the world. And I only wish people in general had the faintest idea of what awaits one here, as, if they had, the world would not be what it is but a great garden of happiness! However, God knows best- and He has not shown it to the world, else people could not but love and follow Him Who came to save us and bring us to the Father. Mr. Taft will know whom he can comfort with these words. My very dearest love to all my own people. Now, sign it only- Archie Butt."

(From my son) "We have never seen anyone more intensely happy on arriving here than was Major Butt."

April 18th, 10:30 P. M:

"Extra" Post announces arrival of the "Carpathia" bearing news that both Major Butt and Mr. William T. Stead went down with the ship.

April 20th, 4 :30 P. M:

(In thinking as to where lay the responsibility for the disaster Captain Smith, himself, testifies, saying:)

"I was responsible, though I could not have averted the accident! I was running too fast, though even if I had been running slower the effect would have been the same. We collided in such a way that the ship was ripped open all her length, and if we had been going slower she would have passed (in) the very same way over the sunken floe that was her death. She could not have stopped even had she been going slowly. The fault was in the ship. No ship of such size is proper to send where there are icebergs. This is my witness... Amen."

April 24th, 4 P. M: Alta Vista, Maryland:

Seated on the porch with my friend, Mrs. A , and

speaking of Major Butt, I received the following:

"I was standing on the deck and I fell forward into the gulf, and when I came to myself I was standing here on the grass with Mr. Stead and several others, and we did not know where we were. We had no idea we had died. We never thought of such a thing. We were simply thunder-struck when some one said, 'We are in the other world.' I think it was Stead who said that. Why, there is no such thing as dying! It is simply marvelous- this passing from the world to the world where we now are."

April 26th, 1912:

While resting this morning after having been down town, I hear the following from Mr. Stead:

"When I crossed the Borderline the first one to welcome me was Julia. It was in a room which I found later was in her house, and she told me of my being on another Plane- or of my having left the world. I knew, of course, that I was no longer on the ship, but would not have realized I had passed from this world had she not enlightened me as to that. Then, at once, she took me out of doors to a place where I found Major Butt and Mr..."

("Mr. Astor?" I suggested)

"No; Mr. and Mrs. Straus. I do not recall seeing Mr. Astor, but there were so many standing there he may have been among the number, and they were all wondering where they were. And then, as Julia had told me, I was allowed to tell them of their whereabouts. I do not know that all of them heard, but Major Butt and the Strauses did at once, and now they are here, and we are all working to help all the others to understand as it is so sad when they will not believe they have left the world, and are so impatient of all counsel and advice, and insist upon being taken to their own homes! Of course they are held back by the wave of grief that has spread over the different countries, and that clogs their minds, and prevents their seizing the Spiritual side of things. But all that will pass. I have been shown that when you publish this many will think as you yourself do, that it is your mind that influences me to say these things, but do not be too much afraid of that influence- it deters many people from hearing helpful things to think in that way."

April 27th:

Upon awaking this morning I heard Mrs. Straus speak to me in the following words: "I am every moment more and more thankful for having come here, as it has given me a wonderful opportunity for helping others. I am as busy as possible, and I pray Our Heavenly Father to show me how I can make things clear to you. That makes no difference; (I had thought of our never having met) All these people who were brought here so suddenly have to be taught, and because of my having always believed in Our Lord and Savior, Jesus Christ." (this astonishes me, as I supposed Mrs. Straus very naturally to be a Jewess.) "I am allowed to show them of His Love. Many know of it, and they learn very quickly, while others are very difficult to teach. I shiver when I think what it would have been if I had remained in the world, and my husband had come here! We both work all the time." ("Helping?") "Of course, we have to find those who are crying and moaning to be taken to their homes, and tell them of their being in another world- a world where, if they wish to be happy, they must turn in prayer to the Father through His Most Blessed Son. I go about and talk and comfort them all I can. It is very much as one would have to do with a parcel of children; but then it is most deeply interesting. Mr. Stead takes another view of things. He wants to get into communication with those in the world in order to help them to understand before coming here, but I think that is a thing very difficult to do, because if they did not believe Our Lord, Himself, how can 'we make them understand.'

You are very much concerned about my not believing in His Name, but I assure you through Christ, Our Lord, that I am one of His followers, and love Him with all my heart, and mind, and Soul, and strength. And now to go back to my work: I certainly count on you, through Christ, to help me to make people understand their continued existence upon passing from the world. Why, every one of us who went down under those icy waters came to themselves just as though they had had a fainting spell, only they awoke- no, that does not describe the sensation at all- they recovered consciousness under many dissimilar conditions.

Some were lying upon couches where they had been put to rest by their Guardian Angels. Some were in lovely gardens with friends they had almost forgotten because they had been taken from the world so long a time ago. Some were on grassy lawns in groups wondering how they came there, and in one of those groups were Mr. Straus and myself. You see, we were together, for which I can never sufficiently thank Our Father. I never thought we could come through so quickly, and stand here at once holding close to one another as we were during our last moments in the world. Yes, it was a terrible moment- but God made it brief. And now we have forgotten all about it, and think only of our happiness at being here together, and of helping so many people who are so sad! That is not all. There is a great work to be done in the world, and this disaster will form, a means by which it may commence. So many now are so anxious to know of the whereabouts of their loved ones who were taken from the world under such trying circumstances. And we want you to help us to show them that we are at no distance removed in any way.

THERE ARE NO DEAD

We see our loved ones in the world; and yet we are never idle for one moment here! I had talked a good deal with Mr. Stead upon this subject, and he was so firm a believer in continued activity of the Spirit that I was almost prepared to find the change scarcely noticeable at first. Our bodies are identical, so far as we can distinguish, with the bodies we had made use of in the world. Our occupations are the same as those we were accustomed to- that is, for many; with some it is otherwise, but I can only tell you of the ones I see! We have each been apportioned to our own homes. We were shown there by friends sent to us for that purpose. My own house"- (here the writer, Mrs. Straus, absolutely refused to continue, and I, greatly distressed, prayed that I might know what had happened. After a moment she resumed her narrative as follows:)

"No one here says my own house- Our home is the loveliest thing I ever saw; so full of lovely flowers and books; and such beautiful chairs to rest on, for we have to rest, and then go out to work again. No! I do not think we eat- I have never thought of that since we have been here- it is a great relief! We read, we talk with our friends, and we go about trying to help the many unfortunates who cannot understand. One thing alone may I tell you more, and that is; that I believe Jesus Christ to be the Messiah we were awaiting- and I am His faithful follower."

(The following is an extract from a letter from one who went down with the ship:)

May 1st, 12 :20 P. M:

"Mr. Stead has brought one whom you can help- it is Mr. C. M.":

"You can help me very much. I have a wife who is so sad I cannot get anywhere near her, and I know if you would only go

89

and talk with her she would feel entirely differently about my going from the world.

It was terrible of course- but it was quickly over! I can't say for how long a time I was unconscious, but when I came to myself I found all my friends with whom I had been traveling standing right beside me. I think they were busy giving me something to restore my consciousness. Then, as I came to, I found that I was in a beautiful garden- nothing seemed strange- in fact, I thought it was a place I had seen before. It never came into my mind that I had passed from the world. On the contrary, I thought I was visiting friends, and that my wife was, of course, also there. When I asked for her I was told she had 'not yet come,' and, at first, I was perfectly sure she would arrive in an hour or so. But finally some one told me, very gently indeed, that I had left the world, had- in fact- died! I simply considered them out of their minds. It was not possible for one to die and yet be sitting there strong and well- and I told them they must not say such things- it was simply blasphemous to jest upon so solemn a subject. I could not believe them at all! Why, death is only passing to a grander, fuller life. How is it people understand absolutely nothing about it? Tell my wife she will never be alone- that God admits of my being near her always, and I can help her in many ways. Our lives are going on together without any separation at all. If she cannot see me, she will feel my presence; and I pray God, Our Heavenly Father, to bring comfort to my wife and to my family through these words."

Disregarding chronological order I will here state what came to me as I read the verdict of the British court of inquiry pronounced on July 30th by Lord Mersay, the presiding Judge. In reading: the words: "In the circumstances I am unable to blame Captain Smith. Other skilled men would have done the same thing in the same position," I hear Captain Smith say: "I thank God for that- I have wished and wished and wished I might

THERE ARE NO DEAD

know how that investigation ended and now I have read it when you read it, and I cannot sufficiently thank God for showing it to me. I don't see how I could have done otherwise than as I did. I had done it hundreds of times before and nothing had ever happened. Every captain who crosses the ocean does it. It is wrong, of course but then it is the custom. Could we know such terrible conditions as had never been known before prevailed? As I said before, those long ships are too unwieldy to use in crossing the ocean or in any other place. Tell them if they use them again there will be just such another accident and they must give them up. No other ship must be built of the size of the 'Titanic' It will be fatal to many more people than were lost on her. I insist upon your publishing this. It is most important. That is all. Smith- late Captain of the 'Titanic.'"

Bethlehem, Pa., June, 1912:

Feeling Mrs. Straus to be beside me, I ask: "If you believe in Jesus Christ, how is it you are still a Jew.?"

A. "I am a Jew as He was a Jew- He was a Descendant of our King David- (He was) our rightful King as well as our Messiah. Many rejected Him but I never did, and I love Him with all my heart. We are the chosen people of God. Why should I cease to be a Jew because I believe our prophecies to have been fulfilled? As He was a Jew I will never cease to be a Jew, and I believe in Him with all my heart and mind and soul and strength. A Jew who loves the Savior can be His faithful follower more perfectly than any other person in the world. That is why I will never cease to be a Jew. I want you to sign it now, from, Mrs. Isador Straus because I wish my husband's name to appear in this also."

THE END

91

Made in the USA
Lexington, KY
26 February 2019